No Man's Yoke
on My Shoulders

OTHER TITLES IN THE REAL VOICES, REAL HISTORY™ SERIES

JOHN F.
BLAIR
PUBLISHER

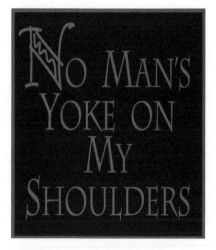

No Man's Yoke on My Shoulders

PERSONAL ACCOUNTS OF SLAVERY IN FLORIDA

EDITED BY
HORACE RANDALL WILLIAMS

Published by John F. Blair, Publisher

Copyright © 2006 by Horace Randall Williams
All rights reserved under International and
Pan American Copyright Conventions

*The paper in this book meets the guidelines
for permanence and durability of the
Committee on Production Guidelines for
Book Longevity of the Council on Library Resources.*

Cover Image: photograph is of Aunt Memory Adams. Aunt
Memory was born into slavery. When she was twenty-four years
old she was taken to Tallahassee and sold to Mr. Argyle for $800.
Aunt Memory attended the 1893 World Fair, and sold enough
photos of herself to pay the expenses.

Courtesy of State Library and Archives of Florida

Library of Congress Cataloging-in-Publication Data

No man's yoke on my shoulders : personal accounts of slavery in
Florida / edited by Horace Randall Williams.
        p.   cm. — (Real voices, real history series)
    ISBN-13: 978-0-89587-285-2 (alk. paper)
    ISBN-10: 0-89587-285-4
    1. Slaves—Florida—Biography. 2. Freedmen—Florida—
Interviews. 3. Slaves—Florida—Social conditions—19th cen-
tury—Sources. 4. Slavery—Florida—History—19th century—
Sources. 5. African Americans—Florida—Social conditions—19th
century—Sources. 6. African Americans—Florida—Interviews. 7.
Florida—Biography. I. Williams, Randall, 1951-   II. Series.

    E445.F5N6 2006
    306.3'620922759—dc22

                                            2005033196

Design by John Tarleton

CONTENTS

Acknowledgments

Like almost everything that happens at NewSouth Books, where I work, the editing of these slave narratives was a team project. My colleague Brian Seidman located several useful sources and obtained library research materials for me. Several interns, including Brenna Weaver, Sarah Harrell, and Kali Pyrlik, typed some of the interviews and corrected proofs. My son McCormick also helped with the proofreading. My greatest help, as usual, came from my partner, Suzanne La Rosa, NewSouth's publisher, who did the preliminary editing on a good number of the narratives and provided encouragement and general support.

I am grateful to Florida historians Ray Arceneaux and Gary Mormino for their advice and for their previous research related to the topic of this volume. Thanks also to Tina Jones of the University of South Florida's Special Collections Department and to Melissa Murnane of the Broward County (Florida) Library.

I am also grateful to the John F. Blair staff. These longtime colleagues make the publishing process look far easier than it actually is. They of course also get the credit for having seen the value to begin with in making the slave narratives more accessible through this series.

INTRODUCTION

This is the eighth book in John F. Blair's series of edited slave narratives begun in 1984 by Belinda Hurmence's *My Folks Don't Want Me to Talk About Slavery*. That first volume focused on North Carolina; subsequent volumes have covered Virginia, South Carolina, Georgia, Tennessee, Texas, Mississippi, and Alabama. Now this one delves into Florida.

The volumes all have as their beginning point the 1936–38 Federal Writers' Project (FWP) interviews with former slaves, most of whom were then in their eighties or nineties and a few even past the century mark. More than two thousand former slaves in seventeen states were interviewed, resulting in about ten thousand pages of transcripts, which were then deposited with the Library of Congress.

The Federal Writers' Project was a part of the Works Progress Administration (WPA), a New Deal program intended to put people to work in ways that contributed to the nation.

Some sixty-six hundred writers, editors, and researchers worked on the project beginning in 1935. They earned only twenty to twenty-five dollars a week, but jobs were so scarce during the Great Depression that most were glad for any work they could get. When federal funding expired in 1939, the project continued on a limited basis with state funding until 1943.

Some Works Progress Administration projects built courthouses and schools, but the individuals involved in the Federal Writers' Project left a different legacy, a significant and wide-ranging exploration of the cultural fabric of the nation. The effort was not universally admired. Some critics thought it was a waste of scarce resources during the bleak Depression years to spend money on intangibles such as art and literature. And Texas congressman Martin Dies, Jr., a 1930s forerunner of Joseph McCarthy, believed the overall Works Progress Administration and the New Deal itself constituted a communist plot. But as historian Gary R. Mormino observed in a 1988 article in the *Florida Historical Quarterly*, "Harry Hopkins, the Roosevelt administration's director of relief programs, quipped, 'Hell, artists have got to eat just like other people.' "

Historian David Brinkley has written that the Federal Writers' Project ultimately published more than 275 books, 700 pamphlets, and 340 articles, leaflets, and radio scripts. Brinkley noted that some of the most significant American literary figures of the twentieth century worked on the project, including John Cheever, Conrad Aiken, Nelson Algren, Saul Bellow, Arna Bontemps, Malcolm Cowley, Edward Dahlberg, Ralph Ellison, Zora Neale Hurston, Eudora Welty, Claude McKay, Kenneth Patchen, Philip Rahv, Kenneth Rexroth, Harold Rosenberg, Studs Terkel, Margaret Walker, Richard Wright, and Frank Yerby.

Alfred Kazin wrote that the FWP began with the mission of inventorying the hardships of the Great Depression but ended up "reporting on the national inheritance" in such a way that it changed the course of American literature. Among the best-known of the project's products is the American Guide Series to each of the states.

Federal Writers' Project interviewers recorded thousands of oral histories, many of which are now available on the Library of Congress's WPA *American Life Histories* Web site (http://memory.loc.gov/ammem/wpaintro/wpahome.html). The interview subjects included poets, novelists, and artists but also laborers, the homeless, and former slaves.

The richness of the narratives and the diversity of voices make the project a unique window into the American past. In the case of the ex-slaves, because few were literate enough to leave written accounts, the interviews are often the only historical record of the thoughts and recollections of those who endured bondage.

Writing for the Library of Congress in its description of the slave narratives, Norman R. Yetman noted that although there exist "several thousand commentaries, autobiographies, narratives, and interviews with those who 'endured' . . . more than one-third are the result of the ambitious efforts of the Federal Writers' Project." Thus the "interviews afforded aged ex-slaves an unparalleled opportunity to give their personal accounts of life under the 'peculiar institution,' to describe in their own words what it felt like to be a slave in the United States."

The interviews were compiled and deposited in the Library of Congress under the title "Slave Narratives: A Folk History of Slavery in the U.S. from Interviews with Former

Slaves." There they lay until 1972, when historian George Rawick edited and published a set of the narratives organized by state under the title *The American Slave: A Composite Autobiography*. This was followed by a Rawick-led project to uncover additional narratives that had for various reasons been omitted from the original Library of Congress collection.

Rawick, in the introduction to *The American Slave*, documented censorship on the part of some of the state project directors of narratives that were "too hot" and were either not forwarded to the central office in Washington or were "toned down" first. In the Florida narratives, this is a complicated and nuanced point. Some historians have been skeptical of the usefulness of the slave narratives because of the suspected influence of the interviewers, especially when, as was often the case, the subjects were elderly, illiterate, poor African Americans, while the interviewers were usually middle-aged, middle-class, educated whites. Thus, while some of the interviewees are extremely candid, one hears in many of the narratives hints of reticence that could have come from fear, nostalgia, politeness, or any number of other reasons. The late historian C. Vann Woodward commented that "the most serious sources of distortion in the FWP narratives came not from the interviewees but from the interviewers—their biases, procedures, and methods—and the interracial circumstances of the interviews." But in Florida, ten of the eleven interviewers were African Americans employed by the Negro Writers' Unit of the Florida contingent of the FWP, and half of those were women.

Andrea Sutcliffe, editor of the Tennessee volume of this series, addressed the issue of interviewer-induced bias in the introduction to *Mighty Rough Times, I Tell You*. She explained that only twenty-six FWP interviews were included in the Library of Congress collection for Tennessee and that part of the reason may be that the Social Sciences Department at Fisk University, the distinguished black institution in Nashville, had already conducted a large number of such interviews in 1929–30. Sutcliffe wrote that the Fisk interviews were different in tone from many done almost a decade later by the FWP. She speculated that the reason was that many of the Fisk interviews were conducted by Ophelia Settle Egypt, a Howard University graduate who was working for Dr. Charles Johnson, a professor in Fisk's Social Sciences Department. "Both were black, and it is possible that the former slaves felt comfortable relating their experiences to a black professional woman who encouraged them to speak about their experiences, good and bad."

Thus it was doubly disappointing to find that the Florida narratives were for the most part rewritten so that the ex-slaves' voices were diluted. In addition, it is impossible to tell from the transcribed narratives where the interviewers' rewriting stopped and some unseen editorial hand began revising. Rachel Austin's interview with ex-slave Douglas Parish, for example, concludes with a third-person passage about carpetbaggers, adventurers, ignorant colored ministers, and "the Negro's unwise use of his ballot." It is hard to imagine Parish, given the context of the rest of the narrative, expressing these political views, and it's equally hard to imagine that these were the views of an interviewer working within the Negro Writers' Unit. It's not impossible, of course, but it is unlikely.

Rawick's ten-volume supplement to *The American Slave* was published in 1979. As valuable as was the original collection, the sheer volume of material made it inaccessible to most potential readers. Belinda Hurmence, editor of the initial volume in the present Blair series, was one of the first editors to distill the material into smaller bites for average readers.

Andrew Waters, editor of the Mississippi entry in the series, retraced Hurmence's steps this way: "Finding the collection of rough drafts, duplicate versions, and third-person accounts unnecessarily intimidating, she decided to pare it down to North Carolina narratives that would be more accessible to the general public. Her 1984 book, *My Folks Don't Want Me to Talk about Slavery*, contained twenty-one narratives selected for their quality. Hurmence's criteria were that the narratives had to be first-person accounts and that they had to contain memories of life under slavery and recollections of the Civil War. The second criterion was necessary because many of those interviewed by the Federal Writers' Project were born just before the Civil War and had no clear memories of slavery."

Waters also addressed a problem he faced in editing the Mississippi volume:

> The major editorial challenge in this collection was the issue of dialect. Dialect was employed heavily by the writers and editors of the Federal Writers' Project, presumably because they felt it was as important to preserve the subjects' way of talking as it was to preserve what they said. Unfortunately, the heavy use of dialect can make the narratives challenging to modern readers. I suppose it would have been possible to correct all the unusual spellings and abbreviations, but that did not seem the ideal solution, since the

manner of speaking is part of the stories. Therefore, I attempted to balance these two issues, correcting obscure abbreviations and misspellings but leaving the unusual syntax intact. Obscure words are often interpreted within brackets, and editorial notes are employed to clarify confusing accounts. Many of these devices were added by the original interviewers and editors. I have also added my own when I felt it was necessary.

I found Waters's summary of the dialect problem apt when I was working on the 2003 volume on Alabama. I may have gone farther than Waters in preserving some of the dialect as reproduced by the original interviewers; Waters himself had gone farther than Hurmence, who seems to have cleaned up her narrators' language more than I felt comfortable doing. I felt that the slight added difficulty of the dialect was more than compensated for by hearing the voices as nearly as possible to how they apparently spoke to their interviewers in the 1930s. However, I did substitute *these* for *dese*, *they* for *dey*, *the* for *de*, and so forth, because those dialect words appeared so frequently that leaving them in seemed a burden that would have unnecessarily slowed reading. I also tried to minimize the use of apostrophes to indicate elisions such as *'em* for *them* and *'bout* for *about*. I simply wrote *bout, em*, and *jes* in instances where I felt the reader would have no difficulty. This editorial method, by the way, is consistent with the "Negro Dialect Suggestions" of John A. Lomax and Sterling A. Brown in the Washington headquarters of the FWP to the interviewers in the various state field offices. Among the suggestions was this: "Do not write . . . *ah* for *I*, *hit* for *it*, *tuh* for *to*, *mah* for *my*, *ovah* for *over*."

That general approach worked fine for the Alabama narratives, where many of the interviews were of high quality and the voices of the narrators rang with authenticity. It didn't work so well with the Florida narratives, which were scant and slight by comparison.

The reason for this presents an interesting challenge of historical interpretation.

One of the issues most, if not all, of the editors of the John F. Blair series have had to wrestle with is that of selectivity. Many of the interviews were with ex-slaves who were in their seventies or early eighties but had been too young at Emancipation for real firsthand memories of life in bondage. Such interviews were omitted, along with those where the interviewee had lived during slavery in a different state from the one for which the immediate volume was being compiled.

In Florida, this approach severely reduced the available material. There are seventy-two interviews identified with Florida in the Library of Congress collection. But when you eliminate those where the ex-slave moved to Florida after Emancipation and those where the speaker was born too late to have firsthand knowledge of life under slavery, fewer than two dozen are left. Gary Mormino has noted that about three percent of the 2,358 interviews in the Slave Narrative Collection were conducted in Florida, but only one percent of the subjects had experienced slavery in Florida.

The paucity of the Florida narratives is disappointing for two reasons.

First, Florida had two aspects of the slave experience that were unique: one, the influence of Spanish governance and culture, which lasted until 1821, and two, the interaction of slaves with the Seminole Indians, who took in runaway slaves and intermarried with them, as opposed to the Creeks and

Cherokees, some of whom themselves became slave owners. Unhappily, there is virtually nothing in the Florida narratives to shed light on either point.

Secondly, one would have expected the Florida narratives to be better in quality and scope than those of other states, since all but one of the interviewers were African American themselves. Also, Florida had an unusual number of African Americans employed within the WPA/FWP ranks, and the administration seems to have been racially enlightened for the period. Zora Neale Hurston not only worked for the FWP but was the head of its Folklore Unit in 1937–38. And FWP state director Carita Doggett Corse and folklorist-author Stetson Kennedy were especially zealous in including African American culture and history.

In fact, Gary Mormino has pointed out that the entire Slave Narrative Collection originated with several interviews of ex-slaves by Florida's Negro Writers' Unit. Those interviews were forwarded by Corse in March 1937 to John Lomax. They excited Lomax, who promptly wrote back to Corse his congratulations "on being the first to open up . . . this field of investigation." Mormino wrote that Lomax "proceeded to draw up a standard questionnaire to get the Negro thinking and talking about the days of slavery."

In hindsight, Lomax's questionnaire may have been more of a hindrance than a help, because many of the Florida interviews go so out of their way to get answers to Lomax's questions that the spontaneity is sucked out of them. Rather than being open-ended, they are rote, as is particularly obvious in Samuel Johnson's interview of Squires Jackson. And rather than being in the ex-slaves' vernacular, they are in the cleaned-up, sanitized language of bureaucratic reports.

Of course, across all the states, the ex-slave interviews are uneven in quality. As Belinda Hurmence pointed out in the introduction to her first volume, the interviewers were "supplied with a list of questions to ask, told to write down the answers as nearly verbatim as possible, and by and large that is what they did. The result is a remarkably eloquent prose."

But not always. Some of the interviewers were quite skillful in their questioning and in the organization and editing of their material. The interviews that work best are those where the former slave is allowed to speak and the interviewer's presence is almost invisible. In others, the interviewer may have accurately captured the speaker's meaning, but the content is rendered in a third-person prose that is flat and passive.

In the Florida narratives, the third-person prose is a serious limitation because there were few interviews to begin with and because almost all were heavily edited into the interviewers' voices. The information is often excellent, but the interviews are usually not as engaging as those in the first person.

Compare, for example, the narrative of Margrett Nickerson of Leon County to that of Claude Augusta Wilson of Columbia County, both discussing the making of lye soap.

Nickerson: "My pa made soap from ashes when cleaning new ground. He took a hopper to put the ashes in, made a little stool 'side the house, put the ashes in, and poured water on it to drip; at night after gittin' off from work he'd put in the grease and make the soap. I made it sometimes, and I make it now, myself."

Wilson, as transcribed by his interviewer: "The ashes were placed in a tub and water poured over them. This was left to set. After setting for a certain time the water from the ashes was poured into a pot containing grease. This was boiled for a certain time and then left to cool. The result was a pot full of soft substance varying in color from white to yellow, and this was called lye soap."

As readers of these interviews today, we feel that we know Nickerson, but we can't feel the same about Wilson.

Additional limitations of all the slave narratives include the age of the interviewees, the hard economic times of the 1930s, and the extreme racial circumstances of the early twentieth century.

To have had useful memories of slavery, the interviewees would have had to be at least eight or ten years old in 1865, which means that by 1936–38, they would have been at least seventy-nine. Many of those interviewed were much older, some past the century mark. They were at an age where nostalgia for the years of their youth would have colored their memories under the best of circumstances.

And circumstances were not the best. In 1936–38, many, if not most, of the elderly interviewees were destitute, often without family, usually without access to medical care, and all too frequently without adequate food, clothing, and shelter. It is not surprising, then, that they recalled the frolics of their youth (or the fact that they had plenty of plantation-grown vegetables to eat, or that their mistress handed down to them fancy dresses on occasion) as vividly as they did the unpaid hard labor of slavery.

In addition, as brutal as they remembered slavery to have been, they had witnessed in their lifetimes the crushing of black political and economic aspirations with the collapse of Reconstruction. And though they had thrown off the yoke of slavery, they chafed under rigid Jim Crow segregation. As Gary Mormino has noted, "Throughout [the 1930s], evidence of peonage, sharecropping, and lynching served notice as to the nature of power in the lower South. Between 1931 and 1935, more than seventy blacks were lynched in the South. Given such a system, the thoughtful ex-slave often preferred to opt for silence or modify what he or she wished to remember. Martin Jackson, an ex-slave, reflected on these problems when he observed, 'Lot of old slaves closes the door before they tell the truth about their days of slavery.' "

Frank Berry of Jacksonville, who was only eight at Emancipation and remembered little of slavery, nonetheless told his interviewer, as quoted by Mormino, "Even in slavery we were treated better than we are now by the white people. . . . Even the white people didn't kill Negroes then as they do now. Anybody can kill a Negro now because they ain't worth a cent to nobody."

Notwithstanding their limitations, the Florida slave narratives are useful to modern readers as both literature and history.

As Norman Yetman has observed, the two thousand-plus slave interviews conducted by the FWP represent the broadest look at the slave experience that exists from the perspective of those who endured slavery. "The treatment these individuals reported ran the gamut from the most harsh, impersonal, and exploitative to work and living conditions that were intimate and benevolent."

So it is with the Florida interviews, which must be read with an eye to all the limitations noted but which can still be appreciated as the best window we have into the way slavery felt and looked and smelled to the African American Floridians who lived under it. Gary Mormino has written, "The enslavement of Florida's blacks ranks as one of the major events in the state's history. Yet the story has not been easy to tell. No Florida slave left behind a diary, and few accounts of planters and mistresses have survived. In order to understand the tragedy and triumph of the freedmen, historians need to examine sources reflecting the views of masters and slaves. The slave narratives constitute the single greatest source capturing the personal experiences of the ex-slave."

In 1860, according to census data, Florida's population was only 140,424, and of those, 61,745 were slaves. That's a large proportion of a small population, which makes the few Florida narratives recorded by the Federal Writers' Project all the more precious and valuable to us today as we try to understand a period in our history when one race of people felt they had the moral right to hold another race of people in bondage and treat them basically as they pleased. The gulf is vast between what we know today and what they experienced then.

The topic of slavery is difficult for modern readers because it is painful and, in the South, at least, remains political. Nearly a century and a half after slavery's end, its legacy is mostly unacknowledged but is reflected everywhere in contemporary Southern life. While the South of the twenty-first century is a world apart from the dark days of slavery and segregation—the region now has more elected black officials than any other, to cite just one example—there is no escaping that the issues of race persist at both the individual and institutional levels.

And today there is the added wrinkle of white guilt on the one hand and white backlash on the other—backlash against such issues as affirmative action, continued federal judicial oversight of local elections, and, more recently, the growing push for reparations.

The Federal Writers' Project interviews go a long way toward clearing up some of these misunderstandings because the former slaves' voices offer direct testimony about what they saw and experienced.

Thus we can rejoice with Squires Jackson, almost ninety-six when he was interviewed by Samuel Johnson in Jacksonville. "No storm lasts forever . . . ," Jackson said. "Even the best masters in slavery couldn't be as good as the worst person in Freedom. Oh, God, it's good to be free, and I am thankful."

HORACE RANDALL WILLIAMS

No Man's Yoke
on My Shoulders

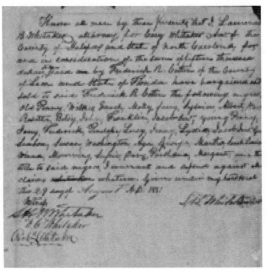

courtesy of State Archives of Florida

CONTRACT FOR SALE OF SLAVES TO A FLORIDA SLAVE OWNER

Know all men by these presents that I, Laurence B. Whitaker attorney for Cary Whitaker Senr. of the County of Halifax and State of North Carolina, for and in consideration of the sum of fifteen thousand dollars to me paid by Frederick R. Cotten of the County of Leon and State of Florida have bargained and sold to said Frederick R. Cotten the following negros: old Penny, Wilkes, Enoch, Molly, Sarry, Sylvia, Albert, Nancy, Rosetta, Betsy, John, Franklin, Jacob Senr., young Penny, Jerry, Frederick, Penelope, Lucy, Jenny, Lydia, Jacob Junr., Guni [?], Seaborn, Susan, Washington, Aga [?], George, Martha, Sarah Louisa Winna, Mourning, Scipio, Davy, Parthana, Margaret; and the title to said negros, I warrant and defend against all claims whatever. Given under my hand & seal this 29 day of August A.D. 1851.

L. B. Whitaker
Witness: S. A. Whitaker, H. C. Whitaker, Richd Whitaker

WHEN THE BIG GUN FIRED

MARGRETT NICKERSON
LEON COUNTY

INTERVIEWER RACHEL AUSTIN WROTE:

Margrett Nickerson, speaking here in her own vernacular, was born to William A. Carr on his plantation near Jackson, Leon County, many years ago. When questioned concerning her life on this plantation, she continues:

"Now honey, it's been so long ago, I don' member everything, but I will tell you whut I kin as near right as possible; I kin member five of Marse Carr's chillun: Florida, Susan, 'Lijah, Willie, and Tom. Course Carr never 'lowed us to have a piece of paper in our hands.

"Mr. Kilgo was the fust overseer I member. I was big enough to tote meat and stuff from the smokehouse to the kitchen and to tote water in and git wood for Granny to cook the dinner and for the sucklers who nursed the babies, and I carried dinners back to the hands.

"On this plantation there was bout' a hunnerd head.

Cookin' was done in the fireplace in iron pots, and the meals was plenty of peas, greens, cornbread, burnt corn for coffee—often the marster bought some coffee for us. We got water from the open well. Jes fore the big gun fired [the signal that indicated the arrival of Union troops and Freedom] they fotched my pa from the bay where he was makin' salt; he had heared em say, 'The Yankees is coming,' and was so glad.

"There was rice, cotton, corn, tater fields to be tended to and cowhides to be tanned, thread to be spinned, and thread was made into ropes for plow lines.

"Ole Marse Carr fed us, but he did not care what and where, jes so you made that money, and when you made five and six bales of cotton, said: 'You ain't done nuthin'.'

"When the big gun fired on a Sattidy me and Cabe and Minnie Howard was settin' up corn for the plowers to come along and put dirt to em; Carr read the free papers to us on Sunday, and the corn and cotton had to be tended to. He told us he was goin' to give us the net proceeds [here she chuckles], what turned out to be the corn and cotton stalks. Then he asked them whut would stay with him to step off on the right and them that was leavin' to step off on the left.

"My pa made soap from ashes when cleaning new ground. He took a hopper to put the ashes in, made a little stool 'side the house, put the ashes in, and poured water on it to drip; at night after gittin' off from work he'd put in the grease and make the soap. I made it sometimes, and I make it now, myself.

"My step-pa useter make shoes from cowhides for the farm hands on the plantation and for ever'body on the plantation cept ole Marse and his fambly; they's was different, fine.

"My grandma was Phoebie Austin. My mother was name Rachel Jackson, and my pa was name Edmund Jackson. My mother and Uncle Robert and Joe was stole from Virginia and fetched here. I don't know no niggers that 'listed in the war. I don't member much bout the war, only when they started talkin' bout drillin' men for the war. Joe Sanders was a lieutenant. Marse Carr's sons, Tom and Willie, went to the war.

"We didn't had no doctors, only the grannies; we mostly used hippecat [ipecac] for medicine.

"As I said, Kilgo was the fust overseer I recollect, then Sanders was next and Joe Sanders after him; John C. Haywood came in after Sanders, and when the big gun fired old man Brockington was there. I never saw a nigger sold, but they carried em from our house, and I never seen em no more.

"We had church with the white preachers, and they tole us to mind our master and missus and we would be saved; if not, they said we wouldn't. They never tole us nuthin' bout Jesus.

"On Sunday after workin' hard all the week they would lay down to sleep and be so tired; soon as yo' git to sleep the overseer would come and wake you up and make you go to church.

"When the big gun fired old man Carr had six sacks of Confederate money what he was carrying with him to Athens, Georgia, and all the time if any of us gals where he was axed him [here she raises her voice to a high, pitiful tone], 'Marse, please give us some money,' he says, 'I ain't got a cent,' and right then he would have a chest so full it would take a whole passel of slaves to move it. He had plenty corn, taters, pumpkins, hogs, cows, ev'ything, but he didn't give us nuthin' but strong plain clothes and plenty to eat. We slept in ole common beds, and my pa made up little cribs and put hay in em for the chillun.

"Now if you wanted to keep in with Marster Carr, don't drap yo' shoes in the field and leave em—he'd beat you. You must tote yo' shoes from one field to the other. Didn't, a dog'd be better'n you. He'd say, 'You gun-haided devil, droppin' yo' shoes and everything over the field.'

"Now jes listen. I wanna tell you all I kin, but I wants to tell it right; wait now, I don' wanna make no mistakes, and I don' wanna lie on nobody. I ain't mad now, and I know ain't no use to lie, I takin' my time. I done prayed and got all the malice out of my heart, and I ain't gonna tell no lie for em, and I ain't gonna tell no lie on em. I ain't never seed no slaves sold by Marster Carr. He was allus tellin' me he wuz gonna sell me, but he never did. He sold my pa's fust wife though.

"There was Uncle George Bull, he could read and write, and child, the white folks didn't lak no nigger what could read and write. Carr's wife, Miss Jane, useter teach us Sunday school, but she did not 'low us to tech a book with us hands. So they useter jes take Uncle George Bull and beat him for nuthin'; they would beat him and take him to the lake and put him on a log and shove him in the lake, but he always swimmed out. When they didn't do that they would beat him till the blood ran outen him and then throw him in the ditch in the field and kivver him up with dirt [to his] head and ears and then stick a stick up at his haid. I was a water toter and had stood and seen em do him that way more'n once, and I stood and looked at him till they went away to the other rows, and then I grabbed the dirt offen him, and he'd bresh the dirt off and say, 'Thank you,' git his hoe, and go on back to work. They beat him lak that, and he didn't do a thing to git that sort of treatment.

"I had a sister named Lytie Holly who didn't stand back on none of em. When they'd git behind her, she'd git behind them; she was that stubborn. And when they would beat her she wouldn't holler and jes take it and go on.

"I got some whuppins with strops, but I wanter tell you why I am cripple today: I had to tote tater vines on my haid, me and Fred'rick, and the hands would be a-callin' for em all over the field, but you know, honey, the two us couldn't git to all of em at once, so Joe Sanders would hurry us up by beatin' us with strops and sticks and run us all over the tater ridge; he cripple us both up, and then we couldn't git to all of em. At night my pa would try to fix me up cause I had to go back to work next day. I never walked straight from that day to this, and I have to set here in this chair now, but I don't feel mad none now. I feels good and wants to go to heaven. I ain't gonna tell no lie on white nor black cause tain't no use.

"Some of the slaves run away, lots of em. Some would be caught, and when they ketched em they put bells on em. Fust they would put a iron band round they neck and another one round the waist and rivet em together down the back; the bell would hang on the band round the neck so it would ring when the slave walked, and then they wouldn't git away. Some of em wore these bells three and four months, and when they time was up they'd take em off of em. Jake Overstreet, George Bull, John Green, Ruben Golder, Jim Bradley, and a host of others wore them bells. This is whut I know, not whut somebody else say. I seen it myself. And missus, when the big gun fired, the runaway slaves come out the woods from all directions. We was in the field when it fired, but I members they all very glad.

"After the war we worked, but we got pay for it.

"Ole man Pierce and others would call some kind of a perlitical meetin', but I could never understand whut they was talkin' bout. We didn't had no kind of schools, and all I knows bout them is that I sent my chilluns in Leon and Gadsden counties.

"I had lots of sisters and brothers, but I can't member the names of none but Lytie, Mary, Patsy, and Ella. My brothers is Edmond and Cornelius Jackson. Cornelius is livin' now somewhere, I think, but I don't never see him.

"When the big gun fired I was a young missy totin' cotton to the scales at the gin house. If the gin house was close by you had to tote the cotton to it, but if it was fur away wagons'd come to the fields and weigh it up and take it to the gin house.

"I was still livin' near Lake Jackson, and we went to Abram Bailey's place near Tallahassee. Carr turned us out without nuthin', and Bailey gived us his hammock, and we went there for a home. Fust we cut down saplins [saplings], for we didn't had no house, and took the tops of pines and put on the top; then we put dirt on top of these saplins and slept under em. When the rain would come it would wash all the dirt right down in our face, and we'd hafter build us a house all over again. We didn't had nobody to build a house for us, cause Pa was gone and Ma jes had us gals, and we cut the saplins for the man who would build the house for us. We live on Bailey's place a long time and finally built us a log cabin, and then we went from this cabin to Gadsden County to a place named Concord, and there I stay till I come here fore the fire [probably the Jacksonville fire of 1901].

"I had twelve chillun, but right now, missus, I can only member these names: Robert, 'Lijah, Edward, Cornelius, Littie, Rachel, Sophie.

"I was converted in Leon County, and after Freedom I joined the Methodist Church, and my membership is now Mount Zion A.M.E. Church in Jacksonville, Florida.

"My fust husband was Nelson Walker, and the last one

was name Dave Nickerson. I don't think I was twenty years old when the big gun fired, but I was more'n seventeen. I reckon I was a little older than Flossie May [a niece who is seventeen] is now."

NICKERSON WAS INTERVIEWED DECEMBER 5, 1936.
RACHEL AUSTIN WROTE IN HER NOTES:

Mrs. Nickerson, according to her information, must be about eighty-nine or ninety years of age. She sees without glasses, having never used them; she does not read or write but speaks in a convincing manner. She has most of her teeth and a splendid appetite. She spends her time sitting in a wheelchair sewing on quilts. She has several quilts that she has pieced, some from very small scraps which she has cut without the use of any particular pattern.

She has a full head of beautiful snowy white hair and has the use of her limbs, except her legs, and is able to do most things for herself. She lives with her daughter at 1600 Myrtle Avenue, Jacksonville, Florida.

INTERVIEWER JAMES JOHNSON WROTE:

In 1857 on the plantation of Tom Dexter in Lake City, Columbia County, Florida, was born a Negro, Claude Augusta Wilson, of slave parents. His master, Tom Dexter, was very kind to his slaves, and was said to have been a Yankee. His wife, Mary Ann Dexter, a Southerner, was the direct opposite; she was very mean. Claude was eight years old when Emancipation came.

The Dexter plantation was quite a large place, covering one hundred or more acres. There were about one hundred slaves, including children. They had regular one-room quarters built of logs, which was quite insignificant in comparison with the palatial Dexter mansion. The slaves would arise early each morning, being awakened by a "driver," who was a white man, and by sunup would be at their respective tasks in the fields. All day they worked, stopping at noon to get a bite to eat, which they carried on the fields from their cabins.

At sundown they would quit work and return to their cabins, prepare their meals, and gossip from cabin to cabin, finally retiring to await the dawn of a new day, which signaled a return to their routine duties. On Sundays they would gather at a poorly constructed frame building which was known as the Meeting House. In this building they would give praise and thanks to their God. The rest of the day was spent in relaxation, as this was the only day of the week in which they were not forced to work.

Claude Augusta worked in the fields; his mother and sister worked in the Dexter mansion. Their duties were general housework, cooking, and sewing. His mother was very rebellious toward her duties and constantly harassed the missus about letting her work in the fields with her husband until finally she was permitted to make the change from the house to the fields to be near her man.

The missus taught Claude's sister to sew, and to the present day most of her female descendants have some ability in dressmaking.

The mansion was furnished with the latest furniture of the time, but the slave quarters had only the cheapest and barest necessities. His mother had no stove but cooked in the fireplace using a skillet and spider [a cooking vessel that sat over the fire on three legs]. The cooking was not done directly on the coals in the fireplace, but [pots were] placed on the hearth and hot coals pulled around them, more coals being pulled about until the food was cooked as desired. Cornbread, beans, sweet potatoes (Irish potatoes being unknown), and collard greens were the principal foods eaten.

Cornbread was made as it is today, only cooked differently. The cornmeal after being mixed was wrapped in tannion leaves (elephant ears) and placed in hot coals. The leaves would parch to a crisp, and when the bread was removed it was a beautiful brown and unburned. Sweet potatoes were roasted in the hot coals. Corn was often roasted in the shucks. There was a substitute for coffee that afforded a striking similarity in taste. The husks of the grains of corn were parched, hot water was then poured on this, and the result was a pleasant substitute for coffee. There was another bread used as a dessert, known as potato bread, made by boiling [sweet] potatoes until done, then mashing and adding grease and meal. This was baked, and then it was ready to serve. For lights, candles were made of tallow, which was poured into a mould when hot. A cord was run through the center of the candle impression in the mould in which the tallow was poured. When this cooled the candle with cord was all ready for lighting.

The only means of obtaining water was from an open well. No ice was used. The first ice that Claude ever saw in its regular form was in Jacksonville after Emancipation. This ice was naturally shipped from the North to be sold. It was called Lake Ice.

Tanning and curing pig and cow hides was done, but Claude never saw the process performed during slavery. Claude had no special duties on the plantation on account of his youth. After cotton was picked from the fields the seeds were picked out by hand, and the cotton was then carded for further use. The cotton seed was used for fertilizer. In baling cotton, burlap bags were used on the bales. The soap used was made from taking hickory or oak wood and burning it to ashes. The ashes were placed in a tub and water poured over them.

This was left to set. After setting for a certain time the water from the ashes was poured into a pot containing grease. This was boiled for a certain time and then left to cool. The result was a pot full of soft substance varying in color from white to yellow, and this was called lye soap. This was then cut into bars as desired for use.

For dyeing thread and cloth, red oak bark, sweet gum bark, and shoemake [sumac] roots were boiled in water. The washtubs were large wooden tubs having one handle with holes in it for the fingers. Chicken and goose feathers were always carefully saved to make feather mattresses. Claude remembers when women wore hoop skirts. He was about twenty years of age when narrow skirts became fashionable for women. During slavery the family only used slats on the beds. It was after the war that he saw his first spring bed, and at that time the first buggy. This buggy was driven by ex-governor Reid of Florida, who then lived in South Jacksonville. It was a four-wheeled affair drawn by a horse and looked sensible and natural as a vehicle. The paper money in circulation was called shinplasters.

Claude's uncle Mark Clark joined the Northern army. His master did not go to war but remained on the plantation. One day at noon during the war the gin house was seen to be afire. One of the slaves rushed in and found the master badly burned and writhing in pain. He was taken from the building and given first aid, but his body being burned in oil and so badly burned it burst open, thus ended the life of the kindly master of Claude.

After the war such medicines as castor oil, rhubarb, calomel, and blue mass [a nineteenth-century medicine now thought to be harmful, possibly containing mercury] and salts were generally used. The Civil War raged for some time, and the slaves on Dexter's plantation prayed for victory of the Northern army, though they dared not show their anxiety to Mary Ann Dexter, who was master and mistress since the master's death. Claude and his family remained with the Dexters until peace was declared. Mrs. Dexter informed the slaves they could stay with her if they so desired and that she would furnish everything to cultivate the crops and that she would give them half of what was raised. None of the slaves remained, but all were anxious to see what Freedom was like.

Claude recalls that a six-mule team drove up to the house driven by a colored Union soldier. He helped move the household furniture from their cabin into the wagon. The family then got in, some in the seat with the driver and others in the back of the wagon with the furniture. When the driver pulled off he said to Claude's mother, who was sitting on the seat with him, "Don't you know you is free now?" "Yeh sir," she answered, "I been praying for this a long time." "Come on then, let's go," he answered, and drove off. They passed through Olustee, then Sanderson, Macclenny, and finally Baldwin. It was raining, and they were about twenty miles from their destination, Jacksonville, but they drove on. They reached Jacksonville and were taken to a house that stood on Liberty Street near Adams. White people had been living there but had left before the Northern advance. There they unloaded and were told that this would be their new home. The town was full of colored soldiers, all armed with muskets. Horns and drums could be heard beating and blowing every morning and evening. The colored soldiers appeared to rule the town. More slaves were brought in, and there they were given food by the government which consisted of hardtack (bread reddish in appearance and extremely hard which had to be soaked in water before eating). The meat was known as "salt horse." This looked and tasted somewhat like corned beef.

After being in Jacksonville a short while Claude began to peddle gingerbread and apples in a little basket, selling most of his wares to the colored soldiers. His father got employment with a railroad company in Jacksonville known as the Florida Central Railway and received ninety-nine cents a day, which was considered very good pay. His mother got a job with a family as house woman at a salary of eight dollars a month. They were thus considered getting along fine. They remained in the house where the government placed them for about a year, then his father bought a piece of land in town and built a house of straight boards. There they resided until his death.

By this time many of the white people began to return to their homes, which had been abandoned and in which slaves found shelter. In many instances the whites had to make monetary or other concessions in order to get their homes back. It was said that colored people had taken possession of one of the large white churches of the day, located on Hogan Street between Ashley and Church streets. Claude relates that all this was when Jacksonville was a mere village, with cow and hog pens in what was considered as downtown. The principal streets were Pine (now Main), Market, and Forsyth. The leading stores were Wilson's and Clarke's. These stores handled groceries, dry goods, and whiskey.

As a means of transportation two-wheeled drays were used. Mule- or horse-drawn cars which were to come into use later were not operating at that time. To cross the St. Johns River one had to go in a rowboat, which was the only ferry and was operated by ex-governor Reid of Florida. It docked on the north side of the river at the foot of Ocean Street, and on the south side at the foot of old Kings Road. It ran between these two points, carrying passengers to and fro.

The leading white families living in Jacksonville at that time were the Hartridges, Bostwicks, Doggetts, Bayels, and L'Engles.

Claude Augusta Wilson, a man along in years, has lived to see many changes, which he is proud of, take place among his people since the Emancipation. A peaceful old gentleman he is, still alert mentally and physically despite his seventy-nine years. His youthful appearance belies his age.

INTERVIEWED IN SUNBEAM, FLORIDA
NOVEMBER 6, 1936

INTERVIEWER RACHEL AUSTIN WROTE:

The life of Florida Clayton illustrates the miscegenation prevalent during the days of slavery. Interesting also is the fact that Florida was not a slave, even though she was a product of those turbulent days.

Many years before her birth on March 1, 1854, Florida's great-grandfather, a white man, came to Tallahassee, Florida, from Washington, District of Columbia, with his children, whom he had by his Negro slave. On coming to Florida, he set all of his children free except one boy, Amos, who was sold to a Major Ward. For what reason this was done, no one knew.

Florida, named for the state in which she was born, was one of seven children born to Charlotte Morris (colored), whose father was a white man, and David Clayton (white).

Florida, in a retrogressive mood, can recall the "nigger hunters" and "nigger stealers" of her childhood days. Mr. Nimrod and Mr. Shehee, both white, specialized in catching runaway slaves with their trained bloodhounds. Her parents always warned her and her brothers and sisters to go in someone's yard whenever they saw these men with their dogs lest the ferocious animals tear them to pieces. In regards to the "nigger stealers," Florida tells of a covered wagon which used to come to Tallahassee at regular intervals and camp in some secluded spot. The children, attracted by the old wagon, would be eager to go near it, but they were always told that "Dry Head and Bloody Bones," a ghost who didn't like children, was in that wagon. It was not until later years that Florida and the other children learned that the driver of the wagon was a "nigger stealer" who stole children and took them to Georgia to sell in the slave markets.

When she was eleven years old, Florida saw the surrender of Tallahassee to the Yankees. Three years later, she came to Jacksonville to live with her sister. She married but is now divorced after twelve years of marriage. Three years ago, she entered the old folks' home at 1827 Franklin Street to live.

INTERVIEWED IN JACKSONVILLE,
NOVEMBER 20, 1936

KIND MASTERS, CRUEL MASTERS

PATIENCE CAMPBELL
JACKSON COUNTY

INTERVIEWER JAMES JOHNSON WROTE:

Patience Campbell, blind for twenty-six years, was born in Jackson County, near Marianna, Florida, about 1853, on a farm of George Bullock. Her mother, Tempy, belonged to Bullock, while her father, Arnold Merritt, belonged to Edward Merritt, a large plantation owner. According to Patience, her mother's owner was very kind, her father's very cruel. Bullock had very few slaves, but Merritt had a great many of them, not a few of whom he sold at the slave markets.

Patience spent most of her time when she was a child playing in the sand while her parents toiled in the fields for their respective owners. Her grandparents on her mother's side belonged to Bullock, but of her father's people she knew nothing.

Since she lived with her mother, Patience fared much better than had she lived with her father. Her main foods included oats, greens, rice, and cornbread, which was replaced by biscuits on Sunday morning. Coffee was made from parched corn or meal and was the chief drink. The food was cooked in large iron pots and pans in an open fireplace and seasoned with salt obtained by evaporating seawater.

Water for all purposes was drawn from a well. To get soap to wash with, the cook would save all the grease left from the cooking. Lye was obtained by mixing oak ashes with water and allowing them to decay. Tubs were made from large barrels.

When she was about seven or eight, Patience assisted other children about her age and older in picking out cotton seeds from the picked cotton. After the cotton was weighed on scales, it was bound in bags made of hemp.

Spinning and weaving were taught Patience when she was about ten. Although the cloth and thread were dyed various colors, she knows only how blue was obtained, by allowing the indigo plant to rot in water and straining the result.

Patience's father was not only a capable field worker but also a finished shoemaker. After tanning and curing his hides by placing them in water with oak bark for several days and then exposing them to the sun to dry, he would cut out the uppers and the soles after measuring the foot to be shod. There would be an inside sole as well as an outside sole, tacked together by means of small tacks. Sewing was done on the shoes by means of flax thread.

Patience remembers saving the feathers from all the fowl to make feather beds. She doesn't remember when women stopped wearing hoops in their skirts nor when bedsprings replaced bed ropes. She does remember, however, that these things were used. She saw her first windmill about thirty-six years ago, ten years before she went blind. She remembers seeing buggies during slavery time, little light carriages, some with two wheels and some with four. She never heard of any money called shinplasters, and she became money-conscious during the war when Confederate currency was introduced. When the slaves were sick, they were given castor oil, turpentine, and medicines made from various roots and herbs.

Patience's master joined the Confederacy, but her father's master did not. Although Negroes could enlist in the Southern army if they desired, none of them wished to do so but preferred to join Northern forces and fight for the thing they desired most, Freedom. When Freedom was no longer a dream but a reality, the Merritts started life on their own as farmers. Twelve-year-old Patience entered one of the schools established by the Freedmen's Bureau. She recalls the gradual growth of Negro settlements, the churches, and the rise and fall of the Negroes politically.

INTERVIEWED IN MONTICELLO, FLORIDA,
DECEMBER 15, 1936

A VOLUNTARY SLAVE

SAMUEL SMALLS/CATO SMITH
SUWANNEE COUNTY

INTERVIEWER MARTIN RICHARDSON WROTE:

The story of a free Negro of Connecticut who came south to observe conditions of slavery, found them very distasteful, then voluntarily entered that slavery for seven years is the interesting tale that Samuel Smalls, eighty-four-year-old ex-slave of 1704 Johnson Street, Jacksonville, tells of his father, Cato Smith.

Smith had been born in Connecticut, son of domestic slaves who were freed when he was still a child. He grew to young manhood in the Northern state, making a living for himself as a carpenter and builder. At these trades he is said to have been very efficient.

Still unmarried at the age of about thirty, he found in himself a desire to travel and see how other Negroes in the country lived. This he did, going from one town to another, working for periods of varying length in the cities in which he lived, eventually drifting to Florida.

His travels eventually brought him to Suwannee County, where he worked for a time as overseer on a plantation. On a nearby plantation where he sometimes visited, he met a young woman for whom he grew to have a great affection. This plantation is said to have belonged to a family of Cones and, according to Smalls, still exists as a large farm.

Smith wanted to marry the young woman, but a difficulty developed: he was free and she was still a slave. He sought her owner. Smith was told that he might have the woman, but he would have to "work out" her cost. He was informed that this would amount to seven years of work on the plantation, naturally without pay.

Within a few days, he was back with his belongings to begin "working out" the cost of his wife. But his work found favor in his voluntary master's eyes; within four years, he was being paid a small sum for the work he did, and by the time the seven years were finished Smith had enough money to immediately purchase a small farm of his own.

Adversity set in, however, and eventually his children found themselves back in slavery and Smith himself practically again enslaved. It was during this period that Smalls was born.

All of the Florida slaves were soon emancipated, however, and the voluntary slave again became a free man. He lived in the Suwannee County vicinity for a number of years afterward, raising a large family.

INTERVIEWED IN JACKSONVILLE,
JANUARY 27, 1937

ON MASTER FOLSOM'S PLANTATION

ACIE THOMAS
JEFFERSON COUNTY

INTERVIEWER PEARL RANDOLPH WROTE:

Mr. Thomas was at home today. There are many days when one might pass and repass the shabby lean-to that is his home without seeing any signs of life. That is because he spends much of his time foraging about the streets of Jacksonville for whatever he can get in the way of food or old clothes, and perhaps a little money.

He is a heavily bearded, bent old man and a familiar figure in the residential sections of the city, where he earns or begs a very meager livelihood. Many know his story and marvel at his ability to relate incidents that must have occurred when he was quite small.

Born in Jefferson County, Florida, on July 26, 1857, he was one of the 150 slaves belonging to the Folsom brothers, Tom and Bryant. His parents, Thomas and Mary, and their parents, as far as they could remember, were all a part of the Folsom estate. The Folsoms never sold a slave except he merited this dire punishment in some way.

Acie heard vague rumors of the cruelties of some slave owners, but it was unknown among the Folsoms. He thinks this was due to the fact that certain "po' white trash" in the vicinity of their plantation owned slaves. It was the habit of the Folsoms to buy out people whenever they could do so by fair means or foul, according to his statements. And by and by there were no poor whites living near them. It was, he further stated, like "damning a nigger's soul if Marse Tom or Marse Bryant threatened to sell him to some po' white trash. And it all brung good results—better than tearing the hide offen him woulda done."

As a child Acie spent much of his time roaming over the broad acres of the Folsom plantation with other slave children. They waded in the streams, fished, chased rabbits, and always knew where the choicest wild berries and nuts grew. He knew all the woods lore common to children of his time. This he learned mostly from "cousin Ed," who was several years older than he and quite willing to enlighten a small boy in these matters.

He was taught that hooting owls were very jealous of their night hours, and that whenever they hooted near a field of workers they were saying, "Task done or not done, night's my time—go home!" Whippoorwills flitted about the woods in cotton-picking time chattering about Jack marrying a widow. He could not remember the story that goes with this. Opossums were a "shamefaced" tribe who "sometimes wandered onto the wrong side of the day and got caught." They never overcame this shame as long as they were in captivity.

When Acie "got up some size" he was required to do small tasks, but the master was not very exacting. There were the important tasks of ferreting out the nests of stray hens, turkeys, guineas, and geese. These nests were robbed to prevent the fowls from hatching too far from the henhouse. Quite a number of these eggs got roasted in remote corners of the plantation by the finders, who built fires and wrapped the eggs in wet rags and covered them with ashes. When they were done a loud pop announced that fact to the roaster. Potatoes were cooked in the same manner and often without rags. Consequently these two tasks were never neglected by the slave children. Cotton picking was not a bad job either—at least to the young.

Then there was the ride to the cotton house at the end of the day atop the baskets and coarse burlap sheets filled with the day's pickings. Acie's fondest ambition was to learn to manipulate the scales that told him who had done a good day's work and who had not. His cousin Ed did this envied task whenever the overseer could not find the time.

Many other things were grown here—corn for the cattle and "roasting ears," peanuts, tobacco, and sugarcane. The cane was ground on the plantation and converted into barrels of syrup and brown sugar. The cane-grinding season was always a gala one. There was always plenty of juice, with the skimmings and fresh syrup for all. Other industries were the blacksmith shop, where horses were shod, and the smokehouses, where scores of hogs and cows were prepared and hung for future use. The sewing was presided over by the mistress. Clothing was made during the summer and stored away for the cool winters. Young slave girls were kept busy at knitting cotton and woolen stockings. Candles were made in the "big house" kitchen and only for consumption by the household of the master. Slaves used fat lightwood knots or their open fireplaces for lighting purposes.

There was always plenty of everything to eat for the slaves. They had white bread that had been made on the place, corn-meal, rice, potatoes, syrup, vegetables, and home-cured meat. Food was cooked in iron pots hung over the fireplace by rings made of the same metal. Bread and pastries were made in the skillet and "spider."

Much work was needed to supply the demands of so large a plantation, but the slaves were often given time off for frol-ics (dances, quiltings, weddings). These gatherings were attended by old and young from neighboring plantations. There was always plenty of food; masters vied with one another for the honor of giving their slaves the finest parties.

There was dancing and music. On the Folsom plantation Bryant, the youngest of the masters, furnished the music. He played the fiddle and liked to see the slaves dance "Cut the Pigeon Wing."

Many matches were made at these affairs. The women came all rigged out in their best, which was not bad at all, as the mistresses often gave them their castoff clothes. Some of these were very fine indeed, with their frills and hoops and many petticoats. Those who had no finery contented themselves with scenting their hair and bodies with sweet herbs, which they also chewed. Quite often they were rewarded by the attention of some swain from a distant plantation. In this case it was necessary for their respective owners to consent to a union. Slaves on the Folsom plantation were always married properly and quite often had a sizable wedding; the master and mistress often came and made merry with their slaves.

Acie knew about the war because he was one of the slaves commandeered by the Confederate army for hauling food and ammunition to different points between Tallahassee and a city in Virginia that he is unable to remember. It was a common occurrence for the soldiers to visit the plantation owners and command a certain number of horses and slaves for services such as Acie did.

He thinks that he might have been about fifteen years old when he was freed. A soldier in blue came to the plantation and brought a document that Tom, their master, read to all the slaves, who had been summoned to the big house for that purpose. About half of them consented to remain with him. The others went away, glad of their new freedom. Few had made any plans and were content to wander about the country, living as they could. Some were more sober-minded, and Acie's father was among the latter. He remained on the Folsom place for a short while; he then settled to sharecropping in Jefferson County. Their first year was hardest because of the many adjustments that had to be made. Then things became better. By means of hard work and the cooperation of friendly whites the slaves in the section soon learned to shift for themselves.

Northerners came south "in swarms" and opened schools for the ex-slaves, but Acie was not fortunate enough to get very far in his "blue-back Webster." There was too much work to be done, with his father trying to buy the land. Nor did he take an interest in the political meetings held in the neighborhood. His parents shared with him the common belief that such things were not to be shared by the humble. Some believed that "too much book learning made the brain weak."

Acie met and married Keziah Wright, who was the daughter of a woman his mother had known during slavery. Strangely enough they had never met as children. With his wife he remained in Jefferson County, where nine of their thirteen children were born.

With his family he moved to Jacksonville and had been living here "a right good while" when the fire occurred in 190[1]. He was employed as a city laborer and helped to build streetcar lines and pave streets. He also helped with the installation of electric wiring in many parts of the city. He was injured while working for the city of Jacksonville but claims he was never in any manner remunerated for this injury.

Acie worked hard and accumulated land in the Moncrief section and lives within a few feet of the spot where his house burned many years ago. He was very sad as he pointed out this spot to his visitor. A few scraggly hedges and an apple tree, a charred bit of fence, a chimney foundation are the only markers of the home he built after years of a hard struggle to have a home. His land is all gone except the scant five acres upon which he lives, and this is only an expanse of broom straw. He is no longer able to cultivate the land, not even having a kitchen garden.

Keziah, the wife, died several years ago, likewise all the children except two. One of these, a girl, is "somewhere up nawth." The son has visited him twice in five years and seems never to have anything to give the old man, who expresses himself as desiring much to "quit dis unfriendly world," since he has nothing to live for except a lot of dead memories. "All done left me now. Everything I got done gone—all except Keziah. She comes and visits me, and we talk and walk over there where we useter set on the porch. She 'low she gwine steal ole Acie some of dese days in the near future, and I'll be mighty glad to go over yonder where all I got is at."

INTERVIEWED IN JACKSONVILLE,
NOVEMBER 25, 1936

ON THE COLONEL'S PLANTATION

DOUGLAS DORSEY
SUWANNEE COUNTY

INTERVIEWER JAMES JOHNSON WROTE:

In South Jacksonville on the Spring Glen Road lives Douglas Dorsey, an ex-slave born in Suwannee County, Florida, in 1851, fourteen years prior to Freedom. His parents, Charlie and Anna Dorsey, were natives of Maryland and free people. In those days, Dorsey relates there were people known as "nigger traders" who used subterfuge to catch Negroes and sell them into slavery. There was one Jeff Davis who was known as a professional "nigger trader"; his slave boat docked in the slip at Maryland, and Jeff Davis and his henchmen went out looking for their victims. Unfortunately, his mother, Anna, and his father were caught one night and were bound and gagged and taken to Jeff Davis's boat, which was waiting in the harbor, and there they were put into stocks. The boat stayed until it was loaded with Negroes, then sailed for Florida, where Davis disposed of his human cargo.

Douglas Dorsey's parents were sold to Colonel Louis Matair, who had a large plantation that was cultivated by eighty-five slaves. Colonel Matair's house was of the pretentious Southern Colonial type which was quite prevalent during this period. The colonel had won his title because of his participation in the Indian war in Florida. He was the typical wealthy Southern gentleman and was very kind to his slaves. His wife, however, was just the opposite. She was exceedingly mean and could easily be termed a tyrant.

There were several children in the Matair family, and their home and plantation were located in Suwannee County, Florida.

Douglas's parents were assigned to take their tasks; his mother was housemaid, and his father was the mechanic, having learned his trade as a free man. Charlie and Anna had several children. When Douglas became large enough, he was kept in the Matair home to build fires, assist in serving meals, and other chores.

Mrs. Matair, being a very cruel woman, would whip the slaves herself for any misdemeanor. Dorsey recalls an incident that is hard to obliterate from his mind. Dorsey's mother was called by Mrs. Matair. Not hearing her, she continued with her duties, when suddenly Mrs. Matair burst out in a frenzy of anger over the woman not answering. Anna explained that she did not hear her call, whereupon Mrs. Matair seized a large butcher knife and struck at Anna. Attempting to ward off the blow, Anna received a long gash on the arm that laid her up for some time. Young Douglas was a witness to this brutal treatment of his mother, and he at that moment made up his mind to kill his mistress. He intended to put strychnine that was used to kill rats into her coffee that he usually served her. Fortunately, Freedom came and saved him of this act, which would have resulted in his death.

He relates another incident in regard to his mistress as follows: To his mother and father was born a little baby boy, whose complexion was rather light. Mrs. Matair at once began accusing Colonel Matair as being the father of the child. Naturally, the colonel denied it, but Mrs. Matair kept harassing him about it until he finally agreed to his wife's desire and sold the child. It was taken from its mother's breast at the age of eight months and auctioned off on the first day of January to the highest bidder. The child was bought by a Captain Ross and taken across the Suwannee River into Hamilton County. Twenty years later, he was located by his family; he was a grown man, married and farming.

Young Douglas had the task each morning of carrying the Matair children's books to school. Willie, a boy of eight, would teach Douglas what he learned in school. Finally Douglas learned the alphabet and numbers. In some way, Mrs. Matair learned that Douglas was learning to read and write. One morning after breakfast, she called her son Willie to the dining room where she was seated and then sent for Douglas to come there too. She then took a quill pen—the kind used at that time—and began writing the alphabet and numerals as far as ten.

Holding the paper up to Douglas, she asked if he knew what they were; he proudly answered in the affirmative, not suspecting anything. She then asked him to name the letters and numerals, which he did. She then asked him to write them, which he did. When he reached the number ten, very proud of his learning, she struck him a heavy blow across the face, saying to him, "If I ever catch you making another figure anywhere, I'll cut your right arm." Naturally Douglas and also her son Willie were much surprised, as each thought what had been done was quite an achievement. She then called Mariah, the cook, to bring a rope, and tying the two of them to the old colonial post on the front porch, she took a chair and sat between the two, whipping them on their naked backs for such a time that for two weeks their clothes stuck to their backs on the lacerated flesh. To ease soreness, Willie would steal grease from the house, and together they would slip into the barn and grease each other's backs.

As to plantation life, Dorsey said that the slaves lived in quarters especially built for them on the plantation. They would leave for the fields at sunup and remain until sundown, stopping only for a meal, which they took along with them.

Instead of having an overseer, they had what was called a "driver" by the name of January. His duties were to get the slaves together in the morning and see that they went to the fields and assign them to their tasks. He worked as the other slaves, though he had more privileges. He would stop work at any time he pleased and go around to inspect the work of the others, and thus rest himself. Most of the orders from the master were issued to him. The crops consisted of cotton, corn, cane, and peas, which were raised in abundance.

When the slaves left the field, they returned to their cabins, and after preparing and eating their evening meal they gathered around a cabin to sing and moan songs seasoned with African melody. Then to the tune of an old fiddle, they danced a dance called the "Green Corn Dance" and "Cut the Pigeon Wing." Sometimes the young men on the plantation would slip away to visit girls on another plantation. If they were caught by the "patrols" while on these visits, they would be lashed on the bare backs as a penalty for this offense. A whipping post was used for this purpose. As soon as one slave was whipped, he was given the whip to whip his brother slave. Very often, the lashes would bring blood very soon from the already-lacerated skin, but this did not stop the lashing until one had received their due number of lashes.

Occasionally the slaves were ordered to church to hear a white minister; they were seated in the front pews of the master's church, while the whites sat in the rear. The minister's admonition to them was to honor their masters and mistresses, and to have no other God but them, as "we cannot see the other God, but you can see your master and mistress." After the services, the driver's wife, who could read and write a little, would tell them that what the minister said was all lies.

Douglas says that he will never forget when he was a lad fourteen years of age, when one evening he was told to go and tell the driver to have all slaves come up to the house; soon the entire host of about eighty-five slaves were gathered there, all sitting around on stumps, some standing. The colonel's son was visibly moved as he told them they were free. He said they could go anywhere they wanted to, for he had no more to do with them, or that they could remain with him and have half of what was raised on the plantation.

The slaves were happy at this news, as they had hardly been aware that there had been a war going on. None of them accepted the offer of the colonel to remain, as they were only too glad to leave the cruelties of the Matair plantation.

Dorsey's father got a job with Judge Carraway of Suwannee, where he worked for one year. He later homesteaded forty acres of land that he received from the government and began farming. Dorsey's father died in Suwannee County when Douglas was a young man, and then he and his mother moved to

Arlington, Florida. His mother died several years ago at a ripe old age.

Douglas Dorsey, aged but with a clear mind, lives with his daughter in Spring Glen.

INTERVIEWED IN JACKSONVILLE,
JANUARY 11, 1937

A Breeder's Son

Douglas Parish
Monticello

Interviewer Rachel Austin Wrote:

Douglas Parish was born in Monticello, Florida, May 7, 1850, to Charles and Fannie Parish, slaves of Jim Parish. Fannie had been bought from a family by the name of Palmer to be a "breeder," that is, a bearer of strong children who could bring high prices at the slave markets. A breeder always fared better than the majority of female slaves, and Fannie Parish was no exception. All she had to do was raise children. Charles Parish labored in the cotton fields, the chief product of the Parish plantation.

As a small boy Douglas used to spend his time shooting marbles, playing ball, racing, and wrestling with the other boys. The marbles were made from lumps of clay hardened in the fireplace. He was a very good runner, and as it was a custom in those days for one plantation owner to match his "nigger" against that of his neighbor, he was a favorite with Parish because he seldom failed to win the race. Parish trained his runners by having them race to the boundary of his plantation and back again. He would reward the winner with a jackknife or a bag of marbles.

Just to be first was an honor in itself, for the fastest runner represented his master in the Fourth of July races, when runners from all over the county competed for top honors and the winner earned a bag of silver for his master. If Master Parish didn't win the prize he was hard to get along with for several days, but gradually he would accept his defeat with resolution. Prizes in less important races ranged from a pair of fighting cocks to a slave, depending upon the seriousness of the betting.

Douglas's first job was picking cotton seed from the cotton. When he was about thirteen years of age he became the stable boy, and soon learned about the care and grooming of horses from an old slave who had charge of the Parish stables. He was also required to keep the buggies, surreys, and spring wagons clean. The buggies were light four-wheeled carriages drawn by one horse. The surreys were covered four-wheeled carriages, open at the sides but having curtains that may be rolled down. He liked this job very much because it gave him an opportunity to ride on the horses, the desire of all the boys on the plantation. They had to be content with chopping wood, running errands, cleaning up the plantation, and similar tasks. Because of his knowledge of horses Douglas was permitted to travel to the coast with his boss and other slaves for the purpose of securing salt from the seawater. It was cheaper to secure salt by this method than it was to purchase it otherwise.

Life in slavery was not all bad, according to Douglas. Parish fed his slaves well, gave them comfortable quarters in which to live, looked after them when they were sick, and worked them very moderately. The food was cooked in the fireplace in large iron pots, pans, and ovens. The slaves had greens, potatoes, corn, rice, meat, peas, and cornbread to eat. The slaves drank an imitation coffee made from parched corn or meal. Since there was no ice to preserve the leftover food, only enough for each meal was prepared.

Parish seldom punished his slaves, and never did he permit his overseer to do so. If the slaves failed to do their work they were reported to him. He would warn them and show them his black whip, which was usually sufficient. He had seen overseers beat slaves to death, and he did not want to risk losing money he had invested in his. After his death his son managed the plantation in much the same manner as his father.

But the war was destined to make the Parishes lose all their slaves by giving them their freedom. Even though they were free to go many of the slaves elected to remain with their mistress, who had always been kind to them. The war swept away much of the money which her husband had left her; and although she would like to have kept all of her slaves she found it impossible to do so. She allowed the real old slaves to remain on the premises and kept a few of the younger ones to work about the plantation. Douglas and his parents were among those who remained on the plantation. His father was a skilled bricklayer and carpenter, and he was employed to make repairs to the property. His mother cooked for the Parishes.

Many of the Negroes migrated north, and they wrote back stories of the "new country" where "de white folks let you do as you please." These stories influenced a great number of other Negroes to go north and begin life anew as servants, waiters, laborers, and cooks. The Negroes who remained in the South were forced to make their own living. At the end of the war foods and commodities had gone up to prices that were impossible for the Negro to pay. Ham, for example, cost forty and fifty cents a pound; lard was twenty-five cents a pound; cotton was two dollars a bushel.

Douglas's father taught him all that he knew about carpentry and bricklaying, and the two were in demand to repair, remodel, or build houses for the white people. Although he never attended school Charles Parish could calculate very rapidly the number of bricks that it would take to build a house. After the establishing of schools by the Freedmen's Bureau, Douglas's father made him go, but he did not like the confinement of school and soon dropped out. The teachers, who for the most part were white, were concerned with only teaching the ex-slaves reading, writing, and arithmetic. The few colored teachers went into the community in an effort to elevate the standard of living. They went into the churches, where they were certain to reach the greatest number of people, and spoke to them of their mission. The Negro teachers were cordially received by the ex-slaves, who were glad to welcome some "Yankee niggers" into their midst.

Whereas the white teachers did not bother with the Negroes except in the classroom, other white men came who showed a decided interest in them. They were called "carpetbaggers" because of the type of traveling bag which they usually carried, and this term later became synonymous with "political adventurer." These men sought to advance their political schemes by getting the Negroes to vote for certain men who would be favorable to them. They bought the Negro votes, or they put a Negro in some unimportant office to obtain good-will of the ex-slaves. They used the ignorant colored minister to further their plans, and he was their willing tool. The Negro's unwise use of his ballot plunged the South further and further into debt, and as a result the South was compelled to restrict his privileges.

INTERVIEWED IN MONTICELLO, FLORIDA, NOVEMBER 10, 1936

INTERVIEWER PEARL RANDOLPH WROTE:

Mrs. McCray was sitting on her porch crooning softly to herself and rocking so gently that one might easily have thought the wind was swaying her chair. Her eyes were closed; her hands, incredibly old and work-worn, were slowly folding and unfolding on her lap.

She listened quietly to the interviewer's request for some of the highlights of her life and finally exclaimed, "Chile, whyn't you look among the living for the highlights?"

There was nothing resentful in this expression, only the patient weariness of one who has been dragged through the boundaries of a yesterday from which she was inseparable and catapulted into a present with which she has nothing in common. After being assured that her life story was of real interest to someone she warmed up and talked quite freely of the life and times as they existed in her day.

How old was she? She confessed quite frankly that she never "knowed" her age. She was a grownup during the Civil War, when she was commandeered by Union soldiers invading the country and employed as a cook. Her owner, one Redding Pamell, possessed a hundred or more slaves and was, according to her statement, very kind to them. It was on his plantation that she was born. Amanda McCray is one of several children born to Jacob and Mary Williams, the latter being blind since Amanda could remember.

Children on the Pamell plantation led a carefree existence until they were about twelve years of age, when they were put to light chores like carrying water and food, picking seed from cotton lint (there were no cotton gins), and minding the smaller children. They were duly schooled in all the current superstitions and listened to the tales of ghosts and animals that talked and reasoned, tales common to the Negro today. Little Mandy believes to this day that hogs can see the wind and that all animals talk like men on Christmas morning at a certain time. Children wore moles' feet and pearl buttons around their necks to ensure easy teething and had their legs bathed in a concoction of wasp nest and vinegar if they were slow about learning to walk. This was supposed to strengthen the weak limbs. It was a common occurrence to see a child of two or three years still nursing at the mother's breast. Their masters encouraged the slaves to do this, thinking it made strong bones and teeth.

At Christmastime the slave children all trooped to "de big house" and stood outside crying, "Christmas gif'!" to their master and mistress. They were never disappointed. Gifts consisted mostly of candies, nuts, and fruits, but there was always some useful article of clothing included, something they were not accustomed to having. Once little Mandy received a beautiful silk dress from her young mistress, who knew how much she liked beautiful clothes. She was a very happy child and loved the dress so much that she never wore it except on some special occasion.

Amanda was trained to be a house servant, learning to cook and knit from the blind mother who refused to let this handicap affect her usefulness. She liked best to sew the fine muslins and silks of her mistress, making beautiful hooped dresses that required eight and ten yards of cloth and sometimes as many as seven petticoats to enhance their fullness. Hoops for these dresses were made of grapevines that were shaped while green and cured in the sun before using. Beautiful imported laces were used to trim the petticoats and pantaloons of the wealthy.

The Pamell slaves had a Negro minister who could hold services anytime he chose, so long as he did not interfere with the work of the other slaves. He was not obliged to do hard menial labor and went about the plantation "all dressed up" in a frock coat and store-bought shoes. He was more than a little conscious of this and was held in awe by the others. He often visited neighboring plantations to hold his services. It was from this minister that they first heard of the Civil War. He held whispered prayers for the success of the Union soldiers, not because Freedom was so desirable to them but for other slaves who were treated so cruelly. There was a praying ground where "the grass never had a chance ter grow fer the troubled knees that kept it crushed down."

Amanda was an exceptionally good cook, and so widespread was this knowledge that the Union soldiers employed her as a cook in their camp for a short while. She does not remember any of their officers and thinks they were no better nor worse than the others. These soldiers committed no depredations in her section except to confiscate whatever they wanted in the way of food and clothing. Some married Southern girls.

Mr. Pamell made land grants to all slaves who wanted to remain with him; few left, so kind had he been to them all.

Life went on in much the same manner for Amanda's family except that the children attended school, where a white teacher instructed them from a "blue-back Webster." Amanda was a young woman, but she managed to learn to read a little. Later they had colored teachers who followed much the same routine as the whites had. They were held in awe by the other Negroes, and every little girl yearned to be a teacher, as this was about the only professional field open to Negro women at that time.

"After de war Negroes blossomed out with fine phaetons [buggies] and ceiled houses and clothes—oh my!"

Mrs. McCray did not keep up with the politics of her time but remembers hearing about Joe Gibbs, member of the Florida legislature. There was much talk then of Booker T. Washington, and many thought him a fool for trying to start a school in Alabama for Negroes.

There have been three widespread "panics" (depressions) during her lifetime, but Mrs. McCray thinks this is the worst one. During the Civil War coffee was so dear that meal was parched and used as a substitute, but now, she remarked, "you can't hardly git the meal for the bread."

Her husband and children are all dead, and she lives with a niece who is no longer young herself. Circumstances are poor here. The niece earns her living as laundress and domestic worker, receiving a very poor wage. Mrs. McCray is now quite infirm and almost blind. She seems happiest talking of the past that was a bit kinder to her.

INTERVIEWED IN MADISON, FLORIDA,
NOVEMBER 13, 1936

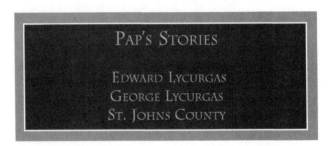

PAP'S STORIES

EDWARD LYCURGAS
GEORGE LYCURGAS
ST. JOHNS COUNTY

INTERVIEWER PEARL RANDOLPH WROTE:

"Pap, tell us 'nother story bout the war—and bout the fust time you saw Mamma."

It has been almost sixty years since a group of children gathered about their father's knee, clamoring for another story. They listened round-eyed to stories they already knew because Pap had told them so many times before. These narratives, along with the great changes he has seen, were carefully recorded in the mind of Edward, the only one of this group now alive.

Pap was always ready to oblige with the story they never tired of. He could always be depended upon to begin at the beginning, for he loved to tell it.

HERE INTERVIEWER RANDOLPH QUOTES EDWARD LYCURGAS
REMEMBERING THE WORDS OF HIS FATHER, GEORGE LYCURGAS:

"It all begun with our ship being took off the coast of Newport News, Virginia. We was runnin' the blockade—sellin' guns and whatnot to them Northerners. We ain't had nothin' to do with the war, unnerstand. We English folks was after the money. Whose war? The North and South's, of course. I hear my captain say many a time as how they was playin' ball with the poor niggers. One side says, 'You can't keep your niggers lessen you pay em and treat em like other folks.' Mind you, that wasn't the real reason they was mad at the South, but it was one of the ways they could be hurted—to free the niggers.

"The South says, 'These is our niggers, and we'll do em as we please,' and so the rumpus got worse than it was afore. The North had all the money, and called itself the Gov'ment. The South ain't had nothin' but a 'termination not to be outdid, so we dealt with the North. The South was called the Rebels.

"So when they see a ship off they coast, they hailed it, and when we kept goin' they fired at us. Twan't long afore we was being unloaded and marched off to the lousiest jail I ever been in. My captain kept tellin' em we was English subjects and could not be helt. Me, I was a scairt man cause I was always free, and over here they took it for granted that all black men should be slaves.

"The jailer felt of my muscles one day, when he had marched me out at the point of his musket to fill the watering troughs for the horses. He wanted to know who I belong to, and offered to buy me. When nobody claimed me, they was forced to let me go long with the other Britishers, and as our ship had been destroyed we had to git back home best we could. They didn't dare hold us no longer.

"As the war was still being fit, we was forced to separate cause a lot of us would cause suspicion, traipsing bout the country. Me, I took off southward and away from the war

belt, traveling as far as St. Augustine. It was a dangerous jour-
ney, as anybody was liable to pick me off for a runaway slave.
I was forced to hide in the daytime if I was near a settlement
and travel at night. I met many runaway slaves. Some was trying
to get north and fight for the freeing of they people; others
was jes runnin' away cause they could. Many of em didn't had
no idea where they was goin' and told of havin' good marsters.
But one and all, they had a good strong notion to see what it
was like to own your own body.

"I felt worlds better when I reached St. Augustine. Many
ships landed there, and I knowed I could get my way back at
least to the West Indies, where I come from. I showed my
papers to everybody that 'mounted to anything, and they
knowed I was a free nigger. I had plenty of money on me,
and I made a big to-do 'mong the other free men I met.

"One day, I went to the slave market and watched em
barter off po' niggers lak they was hogs. Whole families sold
together, and some was split—mother gone to one marster
and father and children gone to others. They'd bring a slave
out on the platform and open his mouth, pound his chest,
make him harden his muscles so the buyer could see what he
was gittin'. Young men was called 'bucks' and young women
'wenches.' The person that offered the best price was the buyer.
And they shore did git rid of some pretty gals. They always
looked so shamed and pitiful up on that stand with all them
men standing there lookin' at em with what they had on they
minds shinin' in they eyes. One little gal walked up and left
her mammy mourning so pitiful cause she had to be sold.
Seems like they all belong in a family where nobody ever was
sold. My, she was a pretty gal.

"And that's why your mamma's named Julia, stead of Mary

Jane or Hannah or somethin' else. She cost me $950 and then my own freedom. But she was worth it—every bit of it! After that, I put off my trip back home and made her home my home for three years. Then with our two young children we left Floridy and went to the West Indies to live. We traveled bout a bit, gettin' as far as England. We got letters from your ma's folks, and they jes had to see her or else somebody woulda died, so we sailed back into the war.

"Freedom was declared soon after we got back to this country, and the whole country was turned upside down. The po' niggers went mad. Some refused to work, and they didn't stay in one place long enough to do a thing. The crops suffered, and soon we had starvation times for bout two years. After that, everybody learnt to think of a rainy day, and things got better."

HERE INTERVIEWER RANDOLPH ENDS THE VOICE OF GEORGE LYCURGAS, THE FATHER, AND RETURNS TO THE STORY OF THE SON:

Edward recalls hearing his father tell of eating wild hog salad and cabbage palms. It was a common occurrence to see whole families subsisting on any wild plant not known to be poisonous if it contained the least food value. The freedmen helped those who were newly liberated to gain a footing. Prior to Emancipation, they had not been allowed to associate with slaves for fear they might engender in them the desire to be free. The freedmen bore the brunt of the white man's suspicion whenever there was a slave uprising. They were always accusing them of being instigators. Edward often heard his mother tell of the "patterollers," a group of white men who caught and administered severe whippings to these unfortunate slaves. They also corralled slaves back to their masters if they were caught out after nine o'clock at night without a pass.

George Lycurgas was born at Liverpool, England, and became a seaman at an early age. Edward thinks he might have had a fair education if he had had the chance. The mother, Julia Gray Lycurgas, was the daughter of Barbara and David Gray, slaves of the Flemings of Clay County, Florida.

These slaves were inherited from generation to generation, and no one ever thought to sell one except for punishment or in dire necessity. They were treated kindly and like most slaves of the wealthy had no knowledge of the real cruelties of slavery. But upon the death of their owner, it became necessary to parcel the slaves out to different heirs, some of whom did not believe in holding these unfortunates. These would-be abolitionists were not averse to placing at auction their share of the slaves, however.

It was on this occasion that George Lycurgas saw and bought the girl who was to become his wife. Both are now dead, as are all of the several children except Edward, who tells their story here.

Edward Lycurgas was born on October 28, 1872, at St. Augustine, Florida, shortly after the return of the family from the West Indies. He lived on his father's farm, sharing at an early age the hard work that seemed always in abundance and listening in awe to the stories of the recent war. He heard his elders give thanks for their freedom when they attended church and wondered what it was all about.

No one failed to attend church on Sundays, and all work ceased in the vicinity where a camp meeting was held.

Farmers flocked to the meeting from all parts of St. Johns County. They brought food in their large baskets. Some owned buggies, but most of them hauled their families in wagons or walked. The camp meetings would sometimes last for several days, according to the spiritual fervor exhibited by those attending.

Lycurgas recalls the stirring sermons and spirituals that rang through the woods and could be heard for several miles on a clear day. And the river baptisms! These climaxed the meetings and were attended by large crowds of whites in the neighborhood. All candidates were dressed in white gowns, stockings, and towels wound about their heads bandanna fashion. Two by two, they marched to the river from the spot where they had dressed. There was always some stirring song to accompany their slow march to the river. "Take Me to the Water to Be Baptized" was the favorite spiritual for this occasion.

As in all things, some attended camp meetings for the opportunity it afforded them to indulge in illicit lovemaking. Others went to show their finery, and there was plenty of it, according to Lycurgas's statement. There seemed to be beautiful clothing, fine teams, and buggies everywhere—a sort of reaction from the restraint upon them in slavery. Many wore clothing they could not afford.

There seemed to be a deeper interest in politics during these times. Mass meetings engineered by "carpetbaggers" were often held and largely attended, although the father of Edward did not hold with these activities very much. He often heard the preacher point out Negroes who attended the meetings and attained prominence in politics as an example for members of his flock to follow. He believes he recalls hearing the name of Joseph Gibbs.

Next to the preacher, the Negro schoolteacher was held in greatest respect. Until the year of the "shake" (the earthquake of 1866), there were no Negro schoolteachers in St. Johns County and no school buildings. They attended classes at the fort and were taught by a white woman who had come from "up nawth" for this purpose. Edward was able to learn very little from his "blue-back Webster" because his help was needed on the farm.

He was a lover of home, very shy, and did not care much for courting. He remained with his parents until their deaths and did not leave the vicinity for many years. He is still unmarried and resides at the Clara White Mission, Jacksonville, Florida, where he receives a small salary for the piddling jobs about the place that he is able to do.

INTERVIEWED IN JACKSONVILLE,
DECEMBER 5, 1936

Son of a Wagoner

Louis Napoleon
Tallahassee

Interviewer J. M. Johnson Wrote:

About three miles from South Jacksonville proper down the old St. Augustine Road lives one Louis Napoleon, an ex-slave born in Tallahassee, Florida, about 1857, eight years prior to Emancipation.

His parents were Scipio and Edith Napoleon, being originally owned by Colonel Jon S. Sammis of Arlington, Florida, and the Floyd family of St. Marys, Georgia, respectively.

Scipio and Edith were sold to Arthur Randolph, a physician and large plantation owner of Fort Louis, about five miles from the capitol at Tallahassee. On this large plantation that covered an area of about eight miles and was composed approximately of ninety slaves was where Louis Napoleon first saw the light of day.

Louis's father was known as the "wagoner." His duties

were to haul the commodities raised on the plantation and other things that required a wagon. His mother, Edith, was known as a "breeder" and was kept in the palatial Randolph mansion to loom cloth for the Randolph family and slaves. The cloth was made from the cotton raised on the plantation's fertile fields. As Louis was so young, he had no particular duties, only to look for hen nests, gather eggs, and play with the master's three young boys. There were seven children in the Randolph family, three young boys, two "missy" girls, and two grown sons. Louis would go fishing and hunting with the three younger boys and otherwise engage with them in their childish pranks.

He says that his master and mistress were very kind to the slaves and would never whip them, nor would they allow the "driver," who was a white man named Barton, to do so. Barton lived in a home especially built for him on the plantation. If the driver whipped any of them, all that was necessary for the slave who had been whipped was to report it to the master, and the driver was dismissed, as he was a salaried man.

PLANTATION LIFE

The slaves lived in log cabins especially built for them. They were ceiled and arranged in such a manner as to retain the heat in winter from large fireplaces constructed therein.

Just before the dawn of day, the slaves were aroused from their slumber by a loud blast from a cow horn that was blown by the driver as a signal to prepare themselves for the fields. The plantation being so expansive, those who had to go a long distance to the area where they worked were taken in wagons; those working nearby walked. They took their meals along with them and had their breakfast and dinner on the fields. An hour was allowed for this purpose. The slaves worked while they sang spirituals to break the monotony of long hours of work. At the setting of the sun, with their day's work all done, they returned to their cabins and prepared their evening's meal. Having finished this, the religious among them would gather at one of the cabin doors and give thanks to God in the form of long supplications and old-fashioned songs. Many of them, being highly emotional, would respond in shouts of hallelujahs, sometimes causing the entire group to become "happy," concluding in shouting and praise to God. The wicked slaves expended their pent-up emotions in song and dance. Gathering at one of the cabin doors, they would sing and dance to the tunes of a fife, banjo, or fiddle that was played by one of their number. Finished with this diversion, they would retire to await the dawn of a new day, which indicated more work. The various plantations had white men employed as "patrols," whose duties were to see that the slaves remained on their own plantations, and if they were caught going off without a permit from the master, they were whipped with a rawhide by the driver. There was an exception to this rule, however; on Sundays, the religious slaves were allowed to visit other plantations where religious services were being held without having to go through the matter of having a permit.

RELIGION

There was a free colored man who was called Father James Page, owned by a family of Parkers of Tallahassee. He was freed by them to go and preach to his own people. He could read and write and would visit all the plantations in Tallahassee, preaching the gospel. Each plantation would get a visit from him one Sunday of each month. The slaves on the Randolph plantation would congregate in one of the cabins to receive him, where he would read the Bible and preach and sing. Many times, the services were punctuated by much shouting from the "happy ones." At these services, the sacrament was served to those who had accepted Christ. Those who had not, and were willing to accept Him, were received and prepared for baptism on the next visit of Father Page.

On the day of baptism, the candidates were attired in long white flowing robes, which had been made by one of the slaves. Amidst singing and praises, they marched, being flanked on each side by other believers, to a pond or lake on the plantation, and after the usual ceremony they were "ducked" into the water. This was a day of much shouting and praying.

EDUCATION

The two "missy" girls of the Randolph family were dutiful each Sunday morning to teach the slaves their catechism or Sunday-school lesson. Aside from this, there was no other training.

THE WAR AND FREEDOM

Mr. Napoleon relates that the doctor's two oldest sons went to the war with the Confederate army, as did the white driver,

Barton. His place was filled by one of the slaves, named Peter Parker.

At the closing of the war, word was sent around among the slaves that if they heard the report of a gun, it was the Yankees, and that they were free.

It was in May, in the middle of the day, cotton and corn being planted, plowing going on, and slaves busily engaged in their usual activities, when suddenly the loud report of a gun resounded, then could be heard the slaves crying almost en masse, "Dem's de Yankees." Straightway they dropped the plows, hoes, and other farm implements and hurried to their cabins. They put on their best clothes "to go see the Yankees." Through the countryside to the town of Tallahassee they went. The roads were quickly filled with these happy souls. The streets of Tallahassee were clustered with these jubilant people going here and there to get a glimpse of the Yankees, their liberators. Napoleon says it was a joyous and unforgettable occasion.

When the Randolph slaves returned to their plantation, Dr. Randolph told them that they were free, and if they wanted to go away, they could, and if not, they could remain with him and he would give them half of what was raised on the farms. Some of them left. However, some remained; having no place to go, they decided it was best to remain until the crops came off, thus earning enough to help them in their new venture in home seeking. Those slaves who were too old and not physically able to work remained on the plantation and were cared for by Dr. Randolph until their death.

Napoleon's father, Scipio, got a transfer from the government to his former master, Colonel Sammis of Arlington, and there he lived for a while. He soon got employment with a

Mr. Hatee of the town and after earning enough money bought a tract of land from him there and farmed. There his family lived and increased. Louis, being the oldest of the children, obtained odd jobs with the various settlers, among them being Governor Reid of Florida, who lived in South Jacksonville. Governor Reid raised cattle for market, and Napoleon's job was to bring them across the St. Johns River on a lighter [boat] to Jacksonville, where they were sold.

Louis Napoleon is now aged and infirm, his father and mother having died many years ago. He now lives with one of his younger brothers, who has a fair-sized orange grove on the south side of Jacksonville. He retains the property that his father first bought after Freedom and on which they lived in Arlington. His hair is white and he is bent with age and ill health, but his mental faculties are exceptionally keen for one of his age. He proudly tells you that his master was good to his "niggers" and cannot recall but one time that he saw him whip one of them, and that when one tried to run away to the Yankees. Only memories of a kind master in his days of servitude remain with him as he recalls the dark days of slavery.

INTERVIEWED IN JACKSONVILLE, NOVEMBER 17, 1936

TURNBULL'S DARKIES

CHRISTINE MITCHELL
ST. AUGUSTINE

INTERVIEWER MARTIN RICHARDSON WROTE:

An interesting description of the slave days just prior to the War Between the States is given by Christine Mitchell of St. Augustine.

Christine was born in slavery at St. Augustine, remaining on the plantation until she was about ten years old. During her slave days she knew many of the slaves on plantations in the St. Augustine vicinity. Several of these plantations, she says, were very large, and some of them had as many as one hundred slaves.

The ex-slave, who is now eighty-four years old, recalls that at least three of the plantations in the vicinity were owned or operated by Minorcans. She says that the Minorcans were popularly referred to in the section as "Turnbull's Darkies," a name they apparently resented. This caused many of them, she claims, to drop or change their names to Spanish or American surnames.

Christine moved to Fernandina a few years after her freedom and there lived near the southern tip of Amelia Island, where Negro ex-slaves lived in a small settlement all their own. This settlement still exists, although many of its former residents are either dead or have moved away.

Christine describes the little Amelia Island community as practically self-sustaining, its residents raising their own food, meats, and other commodities. Fishing was a favorite vocation with them, and some of them established themselves as small merchants of sea foods.

Several of the families of Amelia Island, according to the ex-slave, were large ones, and her own relatives, the Drummonds, were among the largest of these.

Christine Mitchell regards herself as one of the oldest remaining ex-slaves in the St. Augustine section and is very well known in the neighborhood of her home at St. Francis and Oneida streets.

INTERVIEWED IN ST. AUGUSTINE,
NOVEMBER 10, 1936

MASTER LENTON'S SLAVE

BOLDEN HALL
JEFFERSON COUNTY

INTERVIEWER ALFRED FARRELL WROTE:

Bolden Hall was born in Walkino, Florida, a little town in Jefferson County, on February 12, 1853, the son of Alfred and Tina Hall. The Halls, who were the slaves of Thomas Lenton, owner of seventy-five or a hundred slaves, were the parents of twenty-one children. The Halls who were born before Emancipation worked on Lenton's large plantation, which was devoted primarily to the growing of cotton and corn and secondarily to the growing of tobacco and pumpkins. Lenton was very good to his slaves and never whipped them unless it was absolutely necessary—which was seldom! He provided them with plenty of food and clothing and always saw to it that their cabins were liveable. He was careful, however, to see that they received no educational training, but did not interfere with their religious quest. The slaves were permitted to attend church with their masters to hear the white preacher, and occasionally the master—supposedly unbeknown to the slaves—would have an itinerant colored minister preach to the slaves, instructing them to obey their master and mistress at all times. Although Freedom came to the slaves in January, Master Lenton kept them until May in order to help him with his crops. When actual Freedom was granted to the slaves, only a few of the young ones left the Lenton plantation. In 1882, Bolden Hall came to Live Oak, where he has resided ever since. He married, but his wife is now dead, and to that union one child was born.

INTERVIEWED IN LIVE OAK, FLORIDA,
AUGUST 20, 1936

INTERVIEWER ALFRED FARRELL WROTE:

Charlotte Mitchell Martin, one of twenty children born to Sheperd and Lucinda Mitchell eighty-two years ago, was a slave of Judge Wilkerson on a large plantation in Sixteen, Florida, a little town near Madison. Sheperd Mitchell was a wagoner who hauled whiskey from Newport News, Virginia, for his owner. Wilkerson was very cruel and held [his slaves] in constant fear. He would not permit them to hold religious meetings or any other kinds of meetings, but they frequently met in secret to conduct religious services. When they were caught the "instigators"—known or suspected—were severely flogged. Charlotte recalls how her oldest brother was whipped to death for taking part in one of the religious ceremonies. This cruel act halted the secret religious services.

Wilkerson found it very profitable to raise and sell slaves.

He selected the strongest and best male and female slaves and mated them exclusively for breeding. The huskiest babies were given the best of attention in order that they might grow into sturdy youths, for it was those who brought the highest prices at the slave markets. Sometimes the master himself had sexual relations with his female slaves, for the products of miscegenation were very remunerative. These offspring were in demand as house servants.

After slavery the Mitchells began to separate. A few of the children remained with their parents and eked out their living from the soil. During this period Charlotte began to attract attention with her herb cures. Doctors sought her out when they were stumped by difficult cases. She came to Live Oak to care for an old colored woman, upon whose death she was given the woman's house and property. For many years she has resided in the old shack farming, making quilts, and practicing her herb doctoring. She has outlived her husband, for whom she bore two children. Her daughter is feeble-minded—Charlotte's herb remedies can't cure her.

INTERVIEWED IN LIVE OAK, FLORIDA,
AUGUST 20, 1936

INTERVIEWER MARTIN RICHARDSON WROTE:

Beady-eyed, gray-whiskered, black little Shack Thomas sits in the sun in front of his hut on the Old St. Augustine Road about three miles south of Jacksonville, one hundred two years old and full of humorous reminiscences about most of those years. To his frequent visitors he relates tales of his past, disjointedly sometimes, but with remarkable clearness and conviction.

The old ex-slave does not remember the exact time of his birth, except that it was in the year 1834, "the day after the end of the Indian war." He does not recall which of the Indian wars but says that it was while there were still many Indians in West Florida, who were very hard for him to understand when he got big enough to talk to them.

He was born, he says, on "a great big place that belonged

to Mr. Jim Campbell; I don't know just exactly how big, but there was a lot of us working on it when I was a little fellow." The place was evidently one of the plantations near Tallahassee; Thomas remembers that as soon as he was large enough he helped his parents and others raise "corn, peanuts, a little bit of cotton, and potatoes. Squash just grew wild in the woods; we used to eat them when we couldn't get anything else much."

The centenarian remembers his parents clearly; his mother was one Nancy, and his father's name was Adam. His father, he says, used to spend hours after the candles were out telling him and his brothers about his capture and his subsequent slavery.

Adam was a native of the west coast of Africa and when quite a young man was attracted one day to a large ship that had just come near his home. With many others he was attracted aboard by bright red handkerchiefs, shawls, and other articles in the hands of the seamen. Shortly afterwards he was securely bound in the hold of the ship, to be later sold in America. Thomas does not know exactly where Adam landed but knows that his father had been in Florida many years before his birth. "I guess that's why I can't stand red things now," he says. "My pa hated the sight of it."

Thomas spent all of his enslaved years on the Campbell plantation, where he describes pre-Emancipation conditions as better than he "used to hear they was on the other places." Campbell himself is described as moderate, if not actually kindly. He did not permit his slaves to be beaten to any great extent. "The most he would give us was a switching, and most of the time we could pray out of that.

"But sometimes he would get a hard man working for him, though," the old man continues. "One of them used to 'buck and gag' us." This he describes as a punishment used particularly with runaways, where the slave would be gagged and tied in a squatting position and left in the sun for hours. He claims to have seen other slaves suspended by their thumbs for varying periods; he repeats, though, that these were not Campbell's practices.

During the years before "surrender" Thomas saw much traffic in slaves. Each year around New Year's itinerant "speculators" would come to his vicinity and either hold a public sale or lead the slaves, tied together, to the plantation for inspection or sale.

"A whole lot of times they wouldn't sell em, they's just trade em like they did horses. The man [plantation owner] would have a couple of old women who couldn't do much anymore, and he'd swap em to the other man for a youngun. I seen lots of em traded that way, and sold for money too."

Thomas recalls at least one Indian family that lived in his neighborhood until he left it after the war. This family, he says, did not work but had a little place of their own. "They didn't have much to do with nobody, though," he adds.

Others of his neighbors during these early years were abolition-minded white residents of the area. These, he says, would take in runaway slaves and "either work em or hide em until they could try to get north." When the abolitionists would get caught at it, though, "they'd take em to town and beat em like they would us, then take their [farms] and run em out."

Later he came to know the "patrols" and the "refugees." Of the former he has only to say that they gave him a lot of trouble every time he didn't have a pass to leave—"They only give me one twice a week"—and of the latter that it was they who induced the slaves of Campbell to remain and finish their crop after Emancipation, receiving one-fourth of it for their share. He states that Campbell exceeded this amount in the division later.

After "surrender" Thomas and his relatives remained on the Campbell place, working for five dollars a month, payable at each Christmas. He recalls how rich he felt with this money, as compared with the other free Negroes in the section. All of the children and his mother were paid this amount, he states.

The old man remembers very clearly the customs that prevailed both before and after his freedom. On the plantation, he says, they never faced actual want of food, although his meals were plain. He ate mostly cornmeal and bacon and squash and potatoes, "and every now and then we'd eat more than that." He doesn't recall exactly what but says it was "lots of greens and cabbage and syrup, and sometimes plenty of meat too."

His mother and the other women were given white cotton—he thinks it may have been duck [a light canvas fabric]—dresses "every now and then," but none of the women really had to confine themselves to white, "cause they'd dye em as soon as they'd get em." For dye they would boil indigo, pokeberries, walnuts, and some tree for which he has an undecipherable name.

Campbell's slaves did not have to go barefoot—not during the colder months, anyway. As soon as winter would come each one was given a pair of bright, untanned leather brogans that would be the envy of the vicinity. Soap for the slaves was made by the women of the plantation by burning cockleburs, blackjack wood, and other materials, then adding the accumulated fat of the past few weeks. For light they were given tallow candles. Asked if there was any certain time to put the candles out at night, Thomas answers that "Mr.

Campbell didn't care how late you stayed up at night, just so you were ready to work at daybreak."

The ex-slave doesn't remember any feathers in the covering for his pallet in the corner of his cabin but says that Mr. Campbell always provided the slaves with blankets and the women with quilts.

By the time he was given Freedom, Thomas had learned several trades in addition to farming; one of them was carpentry. When he eventually left his five-dollar-a-month job with his master he began traveling over the state, a practice he has not discontinued until the present. He worked "in such towns as Perry, Sarasota, Clearwater, and every town in Florida down to where the ocean goes under the bridge [probably Key West]."

He came to Jacksonville about what he believes to be half a century ago. He remembers that it was "ever so long before the fire" of 1901, "way back there when there wasn't but three families over here in South Jacksonville: the Sahds, the Hendricks, and the Oaks. I worked for all of them, but I worked for Mr. Bowden the longest." The reference is to R. L. Bowden, whom Thomas claims as one of his first employers in this section.

The old man has thirty-two children, the eldest of those living looking older than Thomas himself. This "child" is fifty-odd years. Thomas has been married three times and lives now with his fifty-year-old wife.

In front of his shack is a huge, spreading oak tree. He says that there were three of them that he and his wife tended when they first moved to Jacksonville. "That one there was so little that I used to trim it with my pocketknife," he states. The tree he mentioned is now about two and a half feet in diameter.

"Right after my first wife died one of them trees withered," the old man tells you. "I did all I could to save the other one, but pretty soon it was gone too. I guess this other one is waiting for me," he laughs, and points to the remaining oak.

Thomas protests that his health is excellent except for "just a little haze that comes over my eyes, and I can't see so good." He claims that he has no physical aches and pains. Despite his more than a century his voice is lively and his hearing fair, and his desire for travel is still very much alive. When interviewed he had just completed a trip to a daughter in Clearwater and "would have gone farther than that, but my son wouldn't send me no fare like he promised."

INTERVIEWED IN JACKSONVILLE,
DECEMBER 8, 1936

No Storm
Lasts Forever

Squires Jackson
Jacksonville

Interviewer Samuel Johnson Wrote:

Lying comfortably in a bed encased with white sheets, Reverend Squires Jackson, former slave and minister of the gospel living at 706 Third Street, cheerfully related the story of his life. Born in a weather-beaten shanty in Madison, Florida, September 14, 1841, of a large family, he moved to Jacksonville at the age of three with the master and his mother.

Very devoted to his mother, he would follow her into the cotton field as she picked or hoed cotton, urged by the thrashing of the overseer's lash. His master, a prominent political figure of that time, was very kind to his slaves but would not permit them to read and write. Reverend Jackson related an incident after having learned to read and write. One day as he was reading a newspaper, the master walked upon him unexpectedly and demanded to know what he was doing with a newspaper. He immediately turned the paper upside down and declared, "Confederates done won the war." The master laughed and walked away without punishing him. It is interesting to know that slaves on this plantation were not allowed to sing when they were at work, but with all the vigilance of the overseers, nothing could stop those silent songs of labor and prayers for Freedom. On Sundays, the boys on the plantation would play ball and shoot marbles until church time. After church, a hearty meal consisting of rice and salt-pickled pork was the usual Sunday fare, cooked in large iron pots hung over indoor hearths. Sometimes coffee made out of parched cornmeal was added as an extra treat.

He remembers the start of the Civil War with the laying of the Atlantic cable by the Great Eastern [the huge ship that laid the first transatlantic telegraph cable, though Jackson is confused about the date, which was in 1866, not at the start of the war], being nineteen years of age at the time.

Hearing threats of the war which was about to begin, he ran away with his brother to Lake City, many times hiding in trees and groves from the posse that was looking for him. At night, he would cover up his face and body with Spanish moss to sleep. One night, he hid in a tree near a creek, overslept himself, and in the morning a group of white women fishing near the creek saw him and ran to tell the men. Fortunately, however, he escaped.

After four days of wearied traveling, being guided by the North Star and the Indian instinct inherited from his Indian grandmother, he finally reached Lake City. Later reporting to General Scott, he was informed that he was to act as orderly until further ordered. On Saturday morning, February 20, 1861, General Scott called him to his tent and said, "Squire, I have just had you appraised for a thousand dollars, and you are to report to Colonel Guist in Alachua County for service immediately." That very night, he ran away to Wellborn, where the Federals were camping. There in a horse stable were wounded colored soldiers stretched out on the filthy ground. The sight of these wounded men and the feeble medical attention given them by the Federals was so repulsive to him that he decided that he didn't want to join the Federal army. In the silent hours of the evening, he stole away to Tallahassee, thoroughly convinced that war wasn't the place for him. While in the horse-shed makeshift hospital, a white soldier asked one of the wounded colored soldiers to what regiment he belonged. The Negro replied, "Fifty-fourth Regiment, Massachusetts."

At that time, the only railroad was between Lake City and Tallahassee, which he had worked on for a while. At the close of the war, he returned to Jacksonville to begin work as a bricklayer. During this period, Negro skilled help was very much in demand. The first time he saw ice was in 1857 when a ship brought some into this port. Mr. Moody, a white man, opened an icehouse at the foot of Julia Street. That was the only icehouse in the city at that time. On Sundays, he would attend church. One day, he thought he heard the call of God beseeching him to preach. He began to preach in 1868 and was ordained an elder in 1874.

Some of the interesting facts obtained from this slave of the fourth generation were: (1) Salt was obtained by evaporating seawater, (2) there were no regular stoves, (3) cooking was done by hanging iron pots on rails in the fireplaces, (4) an open well was used to obtain water, (5) flour was sold at twelve dollars a barrel, (6) shinplasters were used for money, (7) the first buggy was called a "rockaway" due to the elasticity of the leather springs, and (8) Reverend Jackson saw his first buggy, as described, in 1851.

During the Civil War, cloth as well as all other commodities were very high. Slaves were required to weave the cloth. The women would delight in dancing as they marched to and fro in weaving the cloth by hand. This was one kind of work the slaves enjoyed doing. Even cotton seed was picked by hand, hulling the seeds out with the fingers; there was no way of ginning it by machine at that time. Reverend Jackson vividly recalls croker sacks [burlap] being used around bales of the finer cotton, known as short cotton. During this same period, he made all of the shoes he wore by hand from cowhides. The women slaves at that time wore grass skirts woven very closely with hoops around on the inside to keep from contacting the body.

Gleefully he told of the Saturday-night baths in big wooden washtubs with cut-out holes for the fingers during his boyhood, of the castor oil, old-fashion paregoric, calomel, and burmo chops [unknown] used for medicine at that time. The herb doctors went from home to home during times of illness. Until many years after the Civil War, there were no practicing Negro physicians. Soap was made by mixing bones and lard together, heating, and then straining it into a bucket containing alum, turpentine, and rosin. Lye soap was made by placing burnt ashes into straw with corn shucks placed into [a hopper]. Water is poured over this mixture, and a trough is used to seize the liquid that drips into the tub, and let it stand for a day. Very little moss was used for mattresses; chicken feathers and goose feathers were the principal constituents during his boyhood. Soot mixed with water was the best medicine one could use for the stomachache at that time.

Reverend Jackson married in 1882 and has seven sons and seven daughters. He owns his own home and plenty of other property around the neighborhood. He is ninety-six years of age and still feels as spry as a man of fifty, keen of wit, with a memory as good as can be expected.

This handsome bronze piece of humanity with a snow-white beard over his beaming face ended the interview by saying, "I am waitin' now to hear the call of God to the Promise Land." He once was considered as a candidate for senator after the Civil War but declined to run. He says that the treatment during the time of slavery was very tough at times, but gathering himself up he said, "No storm lasts forever, and I had the faith and courage of Jesus to carry me on," continuing, "Even the best masters in slavery couldn't be as good as the worst person in Freedom. Oh, God, it's good to be free, and I am thankful."

INTERVIEWED IN JACKSONVILLE,
SEPTEMBER 11, 1937

INTERVIEWER VIOLA B. MUSE WROTE:

Willis Williams was born at Tallahassee, Florida, September 15, 1856. He was the son of Ransom and Wilhelmina Williams, who belonged during the period of slavery to Thomas Heyward, a rich merchant who owned a plantation out in the country from Tallahassee and kept slaves out there; he also owned a fine home in the city as well as a large grocery store and produce house. Wilhelmina was the cook at the town house, and his father did carpentry and other light work around the place.

At the time Willis was born and during his early life, even rich people like Mr. Heyward did not have cookstoves. The only means of cooking was by fireplace, which was wide with an iron rod across it. To the rod, a large iron pot was suspended, and in it food was cooked. An iron skillet with a lid was used for baking, and it also was used to cook meats and other food. The common name for the utensil was "spider," and every home had one.

Willis fared well during the first nine years of his life, which were spent in slavery. He was not a victim of any unpleasant experiences as related by other ex-slaves. He played baseball and looked after his younger brothers and sister while his mother was in the kitchen. He was never flogged.

Wilhelmina saw to it that her children were well fed. They did not sit to the table with the master and his family but ate the same food that was served them. Cornbread was baked in the Heyward kitchen, but biscuits also were baked twice daily, and the Negroes were allowed to eat as many as they wished. The dishes were made of tin, and the drinking vessels were made from gourds. Few whites had china dishes, and when they did possess them they were highly prized, and great care was taken of them.

The few other slaves around the town house tended the garden and the many chickens, ducks, and geese on the place. The garden afforded all the vegetables for feeding Master Heyward, his family, and the slaves. He did not object to the slaves eating chicken and green vegetables and sent provisions of all kinds from his store to boot.

Although Mr. Heyward was wealthy there were many things he could not buy, for Tallahassee did not afford them. Willis remembers that candles were mostly used for light. Homemade tallow was used in making them. The moulds, which were made of wood, were of the correct size. Cotton string twisted right from the raw cotton was cut into desired lengths and placed in the moulds first, then heated tallow was poured in until they were filled. The tallow was allowed to set and cool, then they were removed, ready for use.

In those days coffee was very expensive, and a substitute

for it was made from parched corn. The whites used it as well as the slaves.

Willis remembers a man named Pierce who cured cowhides. He used to buy them, and one time Willis skinned a cow and took the hide to him and sold it. Sixty-five and seventy years ago everyone used horses or mules, and they had to have shoes. The blacksmiths wore leather aprons, and the horses and mules wore leather collars. No one knew anything about composition leather for making shoes, so the tanning of hides was a lucrative business.

Clothing during Civil War days and early Reconstruction was simple as compared to present-day togs. Cloth woven from homespun thread was the only kind Negroes had. Every house of any note could boast of a spinning wheel and loom. Cotton, picked by slaves, was cleared of the seed and spun into thread and woven into cloth by them. It was common to know how to spin and weave. Some of the cloth was dyed afterwards with dye made from indigo and pokeberries. Some was used in its natural color.

Cotton was the main product of most Southern plantations, and the owner usually depended upon the income from the sale of his yearly crop to maintain his home and upkeep of his slaves and cattle. It was necessary for every farm to yield as much as possible, and much energy was directed toward growing and picking large crops. Although Mr. Heyward was a successful merchant he did not lose sight of the fact that his country property could yield a bountiful supply of cotton, corn, and tobacco.

Around the town house Mr. Heyward maintained an atmosphere of home life. He wanted his family and his servants well cared for and spared no expense in making life happy.

As Willis remembers the beds were made of Florida moss

and feathers. Boards were laid across for slats and the mattress placed upon the boards. On top of the moss mattress a feather one was placed, which made sleeping very comfortable. In summer the feather mattress was often removed, sunned, aired, and replaced. In winter goose and the downy feathers of chickens were saved and stored in large bags until enough were collected for a mattress, and it was considered a prize to possess one.

Every family of note boasted the ownership of a horse and buggy or several of each. The kind most popular during Willis's boyhood was the one-seated affair with a short wagon-like bed in the rear of the seat. Sometimes two seats were used. The seats were removable and could be used for carrying baggage or other light weights. The brougham, surrey, and landau were unknown to Willis.

Before the Civil War and during the time the great struggle was in full swing women wore hoop skirts, very full, held out with metal hoops. Pantaloons were worn beneath them and around the ankle, where they were gathered very closely; a ruffle edged with a narrow lace finished them off. The waist was a tight-fitting basque, and the sleeves, which could be worn long or to the elbow, were very full. Women also wore their hair high up on their heads with frills around the face. Negro women right after slavery fell into imitating their former mistresses, and many who were fortunate enough to get employment used part of their earnings for at least one good dress. It was usually made of woolen a yard wide, or silk.

Money has undergone a change as rapidly as some other commonplace things. In Willis's early life money valued at less than one dollar was made of paper, just as the dollar, five-dollar, or ten-dollar bills were. There was a difference, however, in requesting change, and not as much care was taken in protecting it from being imitated. The paper money used for change was called "shinplasters," and much of it flooded the Southland during Civil War days.

Mr. Heyward did not enlist in the army, but his eldest son, Charlie, went. His younger son was not old enough. Willis stated that Mr. Heyward did not go because he was in business and was needed at home to look after it. It is not known whether Charlie was killed at war or not, but Willis said he did not return home.

When the news of Freedom came to Thomas Heyward's town slaves it was brought by McCook's Cavalry. After the cavalry reached Tallahassee they separated into sections, each division taking a different part of the town. Negroes of the household were called together and were informed of their freedom. It is remembered by Willis that the slaves were jubilant but not boastful.

Mr. Heyward was dealt a hard blow during the war; his store was confiscated and used as a commissary by the Northern army. When the war ended he was deprived of his slaves, and a great portion of his former wealth vanished with their going.

The loss of his wealth and slaves did not bitter Mr. Heyward; to the contrary, he was as kindhearted as in days past.

McCook's Cavalry did not remain in Tallahassee very long and was replaced by a colored company, the Ninety-ninth Infantry. Their duty was to maintain order within the town. An orchestra was with the outfit, and Willis remembers that they were very good musicians. Singleton, a Negro who had been the slave of a man of Tallahassee, was a member, and his former master invited the orchestra to come to his house and play for the family. The Negroes were glad to render service, went, and after that entertained many white families in their homes.

The Southern soldiers who returned after the war appeared to receive their defeat as good sports, and not as much friction between the races existed as would be imagined.

The ex-slave, while he was glad to be free, wanted to be sheltered under the wings of his former master and mistress. In most cases they were hired by their former owners, and peace reigned around the home or plantation. This was true of Tallahassee, if not of other sections of the South. Soon after the smoke of the cannons had died and people began thinking of the future, the Negroes turned their thoughts toward education. They grasped every opportunity to learn to read and write. Schools were fostered by Northern white capitalists, and white women were sent into the Southland to teach the colored boys and girls to read, write, and figure.

Any Negro who had been fortunate enough to gain some knowledge during slavery could get a position as schoolteacher. As a result many poorly prepared persons entered the schoolroom as tutors.

William Williams, Willis's father, found work at the old Florida Central and Peninsular Railroad yards and worked for many years there. He sent his children to school, and Willis advanced rapidly.

During slavery Negroes attended church, sat in the balcony, and very often log churches were built for them. Meetings were held under brush arbors. After the war, frame and log churches served them as places of worship. These buildings were erected by whites who came into the Southland to help the ex-slaves. Negro men who claimed God had called them to preach served as ministers of most of the Negro churches, but often white preachers visited them and instructed them concerning the Bible and what God wanted them to do. Services were conducted three times a day on Sunday—in the morning at eleven, in the afternoon about three, and at night at eight o'clock.

The manner of worship was very much in keeping with present-day modes. Preachers appealed to the emotions of the flock, and the congregation responded with amens, hallelujahs, clapping of hands, shouting, and screaming. Willis remarked to one white man during his early life that he wondered why the people yelled so loudly, and the man replied that in fifty years hence the Negroes would be educated, know better, and would not do that. He further replied that fifty years ago the white people screamed and shouted that way. Willis wonders now when he sees both white and colored people responding to preaching in much the same way as in his early life if education has made much difference in many cases.

Much superstition and ignorance existed among the Negroes during slavery and early Reconstruction. Some wore bags of sulphur, saying they would keep away disease. Some wore bags of salt and charcoal, believing that evil spirits would be kept away from them. Others wore a silver coin in their shoes, and some made holes in the coin, threaded a string through it, and attached it to the ankle so that no one could conjure them. Some who thought an enemy might sprinkle "goofer dust" around their doorstep swept very clean around the doorstep in the evening and allowed no one to come in afterwards.

The Negro men who spent much time around the "grannies" during slavery learned much about herbs and roots and how they were used to cure all manner of ills. The doctor gave practically the same kind of medicine for most ailments. The white doctors at that time had not been schooled to a great extent and carried medicine bags around to the sickroom which contained pills and a very few other kinds of medicines which they had made from herbs and roots. Some of them are used today, but Willis said most of their medicines were pills.

Ten years after the Civil War, Willis Williams had advanced in his studies to the extent that he passed the government examination and became a railway mail clerk. He ran from Tallahassee to Palatka and River Junction on the Florida Central and Peninsular Railroad. There was no other railroad going into Tallahassee then.

The first Negro railway mail clerk, according to Willis's knowledge, running from Tallahassee to Jacksonville was Benjamin F. Cox. The first colored mail clerk in the Jacksonville post office was Camp Hughes. He was sent to prison for rifling the mail. Willis Myers succeeded Hughes, and Willis Williams succeeded Myers. Willis received a telegram to come to Jacksonville to take Myers's place, and when he came he expected to stay three or four days but after getting here was retained permanently and remained in the service until his retirement.

His first run from Tallahassee to Palatka and River Junction began in 1875 and lasted until 1879. In 1879 he was called to Jacksonville to succeed Myers, and when he retired forty years later he had filled the position creditably and therefore was retired on a pension, which he will receive until his death.

Willis Williams is in good health and attends Ebenezer Methodist Episcopal Church, of which he is a member. He possesses all of his faculties and is able to carry on an intelligent conversation on his fifty years in Jacksonville.

INTERVIEWED IN JACKSONVILLE,
MARCH 20, 1937

THIS TRANSCRIPT IS INCLUDED IN THE LIBRARY OF CONGRESS'S
FLORIDA SLAVE NARRATIVES, BUT IT SEEMS TO BE FROM THE
FOLKLORE UNIT RATHER THAN THE NEGRO WRITERS' UNIT OF
THE FLORIDA FEDERAL WRITERS' PROJECT. THE INTERVIEW
LOCATION IS LISTED AS EATONVILLE, BUT THE DATE IS NOT GIVEN.
THE INTERVIEWER, WHOSE NAME IS NOT RECORDED IN THE
TRANSCRIPT, WROTE:

Mary Minus Biddie, age one hundred five, was born in
Pensacola, Florida, in 1833 and raised in Columbia County.
She is married and has several children. For her age she is
exceptionally active, being able to wash and do her housework. With optimism she looks forward to many more years
of life. Her health is excellent. Having spent thirty-two years
of her life as a slave she relates vividly some of her experiences.

Her master, Lancaster Jamison, was a very kind man and never mistreated his slaves. He was a man of mediocre means, and instead of having a large plantation, as was usual in those days, he ran a boardinghouse, the revenue therefrom furnishing him substance for a livelihood.

He had a small farm from which fresh produce was obtained to supply the needs of his lodgers. Mary's family were his only slaves. The family consisted of her mother, father, brother, and a sister. The children called the old master "Fa" and their father "Pappy." The master never resented this appellation, and took it in good humor. Many travelers stopped at his boardinghouse; Mary's mother did the cooking, her father "tanded" the farm, and Mary and her brother and sister did chores about the place. There was a large one-room house built in the yard in which the family lived. Her father had a separate garden in which he raised his own produce, and also a smokehouse where the family meats were kept. Meats were smoked to preserve them.

During the day Mary's father was kept so busy attending his master's farm that there was no time for him to attend to a little farm that he was allowed to have. He overcame this handicap, however, by setting up huge scaffolds in the field, which he burned, and from the flames that this fire emitted he could see well enough to do [at night] what was necessary to his farm.

The master's first wife was a very kind woman; at her death Mary's master moved from Pensacola to Columbia County.

Mary was very active with the plow; she could handle it with the agility of a man. This prowess gained her the title of "plowgirl."

Cooking

Stoves were unknown, and cooking was done in a fireplace that was built of clay; a large iron rod was built in across the opening of the fireplace, on which were hung pots that had special handles that fitted about the rod, holding them in place over the blazing fire. The food cooking was done in a moveable oven which was placed in the fireplace over hot coals or corncobs. Potatoes were roasted in ashes. Ofttimes Mary's father would sit in front of the fireplace until a late hour in the night, and on arising in the morning the children would find in a corner a number of roasted potatoes which their father had thoughtfully roasted and which the children readily consumed.

Lighting System

Matches were unknown; a flint rock and a file provided the fire. This occurred by striking a file against a flint rock, which threw off sparks that fell into a wad of dry cotton used for the purpose. This cotton, as a rule, readily caught on fire. This was all the fire needed to start any blaze.

Weaving

The white folk wove the cloth on regular looms [for] dresses for the slaves. For various colors of cloth the thread was dyed. The dye was made by digging up red shank and wild indigo root, which were boiled, the substance obtained being some of the best dye to be found.

BEVERAGES AND FOOD

Bread was made from flour and wheat. The meat used was pork, beef, mutton, and goat. For preservation it was smoked and kept in the smokehouse. Coffee was used as a beverage, and when this ran out, as ofttimes happened, parched peanuts were used for the purpose.

Mary and family rose before daybreak and prepared breakfast for the master and his family, after which they ate in the same dining room. When this was over the dishes were washed by Mary, her brother, and sister. The children then played about until meals were served again.

WASHING AND SOAP

Washing was done in homemade wooden tubs, and boiling in iron pots similar to those of today. Soap was made from fat and lye.

AMUSEMENTS

The only amusement to be had was a big candy pulling, or hog killing and chicken cooking. The slaves from the surrounding plantations were allowed to come together on these occasions. A big time was had.

Church

The slaves went to the "white folk" church on Sundays. They were seated in the rear of the church. The white minister would arise and exhort the slaves to "mind your masters; you owe them your respect." An old Christian slave who perceived things differently could sometimes be heard to mumble, "Yeah, we's jest as good as dey is, only dey's white and we's black, huh." She dare not let the whites hear this. At times meetings were held in a slave cabin, where some "inspired" slave led the services.

Mrs. Jamison

In the course of years Mr. Jamison married again. His second wife was a veritable terror. She was always ready and anxious to whip a slave for the least misdemeanor. The master told Mary and her mother that before he would take the chance of them running away on account of her meanness he would leave her. As soon as he would leave the house this was a signal for his wife to start on a slave. One day, with a kettle of hot water in her hand, she chased Mary, who ran to another plantation and hid there until the good master returned. She then poured out her trouble to him. He was very indignant and remonstrated with his wife for being so cruel. She met her fate in later years; her son-in-law, becoming angry at some of her doings in regard to him, shot her, which resulted in her death. Instead of mourning, everybody seemed to rejoice, for the menace to well-being had been removed.

Twice a year Mary's father and master went to Cedar Key, Florida, to get salt. Ocean water was obtained and boiled, salt resulting. They always returned with about three barrels of salt.

FREEDOM

The greatest event in the life of a slave was about to occur, and the most sorrowful in the life of a master. Freedom was at hand. A Negro was seen coming in the distance, mounted upon a mule, approaching Mr. Jamison, who stood upon the porch. He told him of the liberation of the slaves. Mr. Jamison had never before been heard to curse, but this was one day that he let go a torrent of words that are unworthy to appear in print. He then broke down and cried like a slave who was being lashed by his cruel master. He called Mary's mother and father, Phyliss and Sandy. "I ain't got no more to do with you, you are free," he said. "If you want to stay with me you may, and I'll give you one-third of what you raise." They decided to stay. When the crop was harvested the master did not do as he had promised. He gave them nothing. Mary slipped away, mounted the old mule Mustang, and galloped away at a mule's snail speed to Newnansville, where she related what had happened to a Union captain. He gave her a letter to give to Mr. Jamison. In it he reminded him that if he didn't give Mary's family what he had promised he would be put in jail. Without hesitation the old master complied with these pungent orders.

After this incident Mary and her family left the good old boss to seek a new abode in other parts. This was the first time that the master had in any way displayed any kind of unfairness toward them; perhaps it was the reaction to having to liberate them.

Marriage

There was no marriage during slavery, according to civil or religious custom among the slaves. If a slave saw a woman whom he desired he told his master. If the woman in question belonged on another plantation the master would consult her master. "One of my boys wants to marry one of your gals," he would say. As a rule it was agreeable that they should live together as man and wife. This was encouraged, for it increased the slave population by newborns, hence being an asset to the masters. The two slaves thus joined were allowed to see one another at intervals upon special permission from the master. He must have a pass to leave the plantation. Any slave caught without one while off the plantation was subject to be caught by the "patterollers," a low class of white who roved the country to molest slaves at the least opportunity; some were hired by the masters to guard against slaves running away or to apprehend them in the event that they did. They would beat the slaves unmercifully and send them back to the plantation from whence they came.

As a result of this form of matrimony at Emancipation there were no slaves lawfully married. Orders were given that if they preferred to live together as man and wife they must marry according to law. They were given nine months to decide this question, after which if they continued to live together they were arrested for adultery. A Mr. Fryer, justice of the peace at Gainesville, was assigned to deal with the situation around the plantation where Mary and her family lived. A big supper was given. It was early, and about twenty-five slave couples attended. There was gaiety and laughter. A barrel of lemonade was served. A big time was had by all, then those couples who desired to remain together were joined in wedlock according to civil custom. The party broke up in the early hours of the morning.

LIGHTING

Mary Biddie, cognizant of the progress that science and invention have made in the intervening years from Emancipation and the present time, could not help but remark of the vast improvement of the lighting system of today over that of slavery. There were no lamps or kerosene. The first thread that she ever spun was for a wick to be used in a candle, the only means of light. Beef tallow was used to make the candle; this was placed in a candle mould while hot. The wick was then placed in the center of the tallow as it rested in the mould; this was allowed to cool. When this chemical process occurred there was a regular-sized candle to be used for lighting.

ROOSEVELT

Mary, now past the century mark, her lean bronze body resting in a rocker, her head wrapped in a white kerchief and puffing slowly on her clay pipe, expressed herself in regard to presidents: "Roosevelt has done mo' than any other president. Why, you know, ever since Freedom they been talkin' bout dis pension—talkin' bout it, that's all. But, you see, Mr. Roosevelt, he done come and gived it to us. What? I'll say he's a good righteous man, and I'm sho gone vote for him."

Residing in her little cabin in Eatonville, Florida, she is able to smile because she has some means of security, the old-age pension.

Haints

Josephine Anderson
Tampa

This Is Another Interview Included among the Library of Congress's Florida Slave Narratives That Is Apparently from the Folklore Unit Rather Than the Negro Writers' Unit. Interviewer Jules Frost Transcribed Anderson's Words As:

I can't tell nothin' bout slavery times cept what I heared folks talk about. I was too young to remember much, but I recollect seein' my grandma milk the cows and do the washin'. Grampa was old, and they let him do light work, mostly fish and hunt.

I don't member nothin' bout my daddy. He died when I was a baby. My stepfather was Stephen Anderson, and my mammy's name was Dorcas. He come from Vajinny, but my mammy was borned and raised in Wilmington. My name was Josephine Anderson fore I married Willie Jones. I had two half-brothers younger'n me, John Henry and Ed, and a half-sister, Elsie. The boys had to mind the calves and sheeps, and Elsie nursed the missus' baby. I done the cookin', mostly, and helped my mammy spin.

I was only five year old when they brung me to Sanderson, in Baker County, Florida. My stepfather went to work for a turpentine man, makin' barrels, and he work at that job till he drop dead in the camp. I reckon he musta had heart disease.

I don't recollect ever seein' my mammy wear shoes. Even in the winter she go barefoot, and I reckon cold didn't hurt her feet no more'n her hands and face. We all wore dresses made o' homespun. The thread was spun and the cloth wove right in our own home. My mammy and granmammy and me done it in spare time.

My weddin' dress was blue—blue for true. I thought it was the prettiest dress I ever see. We was married in the court-house, and that be a mighty happy day for me. Most folks them days got married by layin' a broom on the floor and jumpin' over it. That seals the marriage and at the same time brings em good luck.

You see, brooms keeps haints away. When mean folks dies the old debbil sometimes don't want em down there in the bad place, so he makes witches out of em and sends em back. One thing bout witches, they gotta count everything fore they can git across it. You put a broom acrost your door at night, an old witch's gotta count ever straw in that broom fore she can come in.

Some folks can jes nachly see haints better'n others. Teeny, my gal, can. I reckon that's cause she been borned with a veil—you know, a caul, what be over some babies' faces when they is borned. Folks borned with a caul can see apperits [apparitions] and tell what's gonna happen fore it comes true.

Use to worry Teeny right smart, seein' apperits day and night. My husband say he gonna cure her, so he taken a grain o' corn and put it in a bottle in Teeny's bedroom overnight. Then he planted it in the yard and drove plenty sticks round the place. When it was growin' good he put leaf mold round the stalk and watch over it ever day and tell us don't nobody touch the stalk. It raises three big ears o' corn, and when they was good roastin' size he pick em off and cook em and tell Teeny eat ever grain offen all three cobs. He watch her while she done it, and she ain't never been worried with haints no more. She sees em jes the same, but they don't bother her none.

Fust time I ever knowed a hant to come into our quarters was when I was jes big enough to go out to parties. The game what we use to play was spin the plate. Ever time I think on that game it gives me the shivers. One time there was a strange young man come to a party where I was. Said he name Richard Green, and he been takin' keer o' horses for a rich man what was gonna buy a plantation in that county. He look kinda slick and dressed up—different from the rest. All the gals begin to cast sheep's eyes at him and hope he gonna choose them when they start playin' games.

Pretty soon they begin to play spin the plate, and it come my turn fust thing. I spin it and call out, "Mr. Green!" He jumps to the middle o' the ring to grab the plate and bang—bout four guns go off all at oncet, and Mr. Green fall to the floor plumb dead, shot through the head.

Fore we knowed who done it the sheriff and some more men jump down from the loft where they been hidin' and tell us to quit hollerin' and don't be scairt. This man be a bad deeper—you know, one o' them outlaws what kills folks. He some kinda foreigner and jes tryin' make believe he a nigger, so's they don't find him.

Well, we didn't feel like playin' no more games, and f'ever after that you couldn't git no niggers to pass that house alone after dark. They say the place was hainted, and if you look through the winder any dark night you could see a man in there spinnin' the plate. I sho didn't never look in, cause I done seen more haints already than I ever want to see again.

One night I was goin' to my granny's house. It was jes comin' dark, and when I get to the crick and start across on the foot log there on the other end o' that log was a man with his haid cut off and layin' plumb over his shoulder. He look at me kinda pitiful and don't say a word—but I closely never waited to see what he gonna talk about. I pure flew back home. I was so scairt I couldn't tell the folks what done happened till I set down and got my breath.

'Nother time not so long ago, when I live down in Gary, I be walkin' down the railroad track soon in the mornin', and fore I knowed it there was a white man walkin' long side o' me. I jes thought it were somebody, but I wudn't sho, so I turn off at the fust street to git way from there. The next mornin' I be goin' to work at the same time. It were kinda foggy and dark, so I never seen nobody till I mighty nigh run into this same man, and there he goes, bout half a step ahead o' me, his two hands restin' on his behind.

I was so close up to him I could see him plain as I see you. He had fingernails that long, all cleaned and polished. He was tall and had on a derby hat and stylish black clothes. When I walk slow he slow down. When I stop he stop, never oncet lookin' round. My feets make a noise on the cinders tween the rails, but he don't make a mite o' noise. That was the fust thing got me scairt, but I figger I better find out for sho ifen he be a spirit, so I say, good and loud, "Looky here, mister, I jes an old colored woman, and I know my place, and I wisht you wouldn't walk with me, counta [what] folks might say."

He never looked round no more'n if I wasn't there, and I cut my eyes round to see if there is somebody I can holler to for help. When I looked back he was gone—gone like that, without makin' a sound. Then I knowed he be a hant, and the next day when I tell somebody bout it they say he be the gen'lman what got killed at the crossin' a spell back, and other folks has seen him jus like I did. They say they can hear babies cryin' at the trestle right near there, and ain't nobody yit ever found em.

That ain't the only hant I ever seen. One day I go out to the smokehouse to git a mess o' taters. It was after sundown but still purty light. When I gits there the door be unlocked and a big man standin' half inside. "What you doin' stealin' our taters!" I holler at him, and—pow!—he gone, jes like that. Did I git back to that house! We mighty glad to eat grits and cornbread that night.

When we livin' at Titusville I see my mammy comin' up the road jes as plain as day. I stand on the porch fixin' to run and meet her, when all of a sudden she be gone. I begin to cry and tell the folks I ain't gonna see my mammy agin. And sho nuff I never did. She die at Sanderson, back in West Florida, fore I got to see her.

Does I believe in witches? Say, I know more bout em than to jes believe—I been rid by em, right here in this house. You ain't never been rid by a witch? Well, you mighty lucky. They come in the night, gen'ly soon after you drop off to sleep. They put a bridle on your head and a bit in your mouth and a saddle on your back. Then they take off their skin and hang it up on the wall. Then they git on you, and some nights they like to ride you to death. You try to holler but you can't, counta the iron bit in your mouth, and you feel like somebody holdin' you down. Then they ride you back home into your bed. When you hit the bed you jump and grab the covers, and the witch be gone, like that. But you know you been rid mighty hard cause you all wet with sweat and you feel plumb tired out. Some folks say you jes been dreamin', counta the blood stop circulatin' in your back. Shucks! They ain't never been rid by a witch, or they ain't sayin' that.

Old witch doctor, he want ten dollars for a piece o' string, what he say some kinda charm words over. Tells me to make a image o' that old witch outa dough and tie that string round its neck. Then when I bake it in the oven, it swell up and the magic string shet off her breath. I didn't have no ten dollars, so he say ifen I git up five dollar he make me a hand—you know, what colored folks calls a jack. That be a charm what will keep the witches away. I knows how to make em, but they don't do no good without the magic words, and I don't know em. You take a little pinch o' dried snakeskin and some graveyard dirt and some red pepper and a lock o' your hair wrapped round some black rooster feathers. Then you spit whiskey on em and wrap em in red flannel and sew it into a ball bout that big. Then you hang it under your right armpit, and ever week you give it a drink o' whiskey to keep it strong and powerful. That keep the witches from ridin' you.

But nary one o' these charms work with this old witch. I got a purty good idee who she is, and she got a charm powerfuller than both of them. But she can't git acrost flax-seed, not till she count ever seed. I gits me a li'l bag o' pure fresh flaxseed, and I sprinkle it all round the bed, then I put some on top of the mattress and under the sheet. Then I goes to bed and sleeps like a baby, and that witch don't bother me no more.

Only oncet, soon's I wake up, I light me a lamp and look on the floor and there, side o' my bed, was my dress, layin' right over that flaxseed so's she could walk over on the dress, big as life. I snatch up the dress and throw it on the bed, then I go to sleep, and I never been bothered no more.

Some folks reads the Bible backwards to keep witches from ridin' em, but that don't do me no good cause I can't read. But flaxseed work so good I don't be studyin' night-ridin' witches no more.

INTERVIEWED IN TAMPA,
OCTOBER 20, 1937

ANNA SCOTT, LIKE MORE THAN HALF OF THE EX-SLAVES
INTERVIEWED IN FLORIDA, WAS A SLAVE ELSEWHERE AND MOVED
TO FLORIDA AFTER EMANCIPATION. EXCEPT FOR SCOTT'S, THE
NON-FLORIDA NARRATIVES WERE OMITTED FROM THIS BOOK.
SCOTT'S IS INCLUDED BECAUSE SHE UNIQUELY ADDRESSED THE
POST-CIVIL WAR EXPERIMENT BY SOME AFRICAN AMERICANS TO
RETURN TO AFRICA. INTERVIEWER VIOLA B. MUSE WROTE:

Anna Scott was a member of one of the first colonization
groups that went to the west coast of Africa following the
emancipation of the slaves in this country.

The former slave was born at Dave City, South Carolina,
on January 28, 1846, of a half-breed Cherokee and Negro
mother and an Anglo-Saxon father. Her father owned the
plantation adjoining that of her master.

Elias Mumford was Anna's stepfather in Charleston, and with him the entire family joined a colonizing expedition to West Africa. There were 650 in the expedition, and it left in 1867. Transportation was free.

The trip took several weeks, but finally the small ship landed at Bassa [perhaps in Guinea]. Mumford did not like the place, however, and continued on to Monrovia, Liberia. He did not like Monrovia either and tried several other ports before being told that he would have to get off anyway. This was at Harper Cape [Liberia], West Africa.

Here he almost immediately began an industry that was to prove lucrative. Oysters were as "large as saucers," according to Anna, and while the family gathered these he would burn and extract lime from them. This he mixed with the native clay and made brick. In addition to his brick-making Mumford cut trees for lumber and with his own brick and lumber would construct houses. One such structure brought him eleven hundred dollars.

Another manner in which Mumford added to his growing wealth was through the cashing of checks for the missionaries of the section. Ordinarily they would have to send these back to the United States to be cashed, and when he offered to cash them at a discount they eagerly utilized the opportunity to save time; this was a convenience for them and more wealth for Mumford.

Anna found other things besides happiness in her eight years in Africa. There were death, sickness, and pestilences. She mentions among the latter the African ants, some of which reached huge proportions. Most dreaded were the mission ants, which infected every house, building, and structure. Sometimes buildings had to be burned to get rid of them. The bite of these ants was so serious that after sixty years Anna still exhibits places on her feet where the ants left their indelible traces.

Another of the pests was the driver ant, so large, powerful, and stubborn that even bodies of water did not stop them. They would join together above the surface of the water and serve as bridges for the passage of the other ants. The driver ants moved in swarms, and their approach could be seen at great distances. When they were seen to be coming toward a settlement the natives would close their doors and windows and build fires around their homes to avoid them. These fires had to be kept burning for weeks.

Eight and more persons died a day from the African fever during the early colonization attempts; three in Anna's family were victims of it. It was generally believed that if a victim of the fever became wet by day he was sure to die.

After eight years Mumford and the remainder of his family returned to America, where the accrued checks he possessed for cashing made him reasonably wealthy. Anna married Robert Scott and moved to Jacksonville, where she has lived since.

At ninety-one she still occupies the little farm on the outskirts of Jacksonville that was purchased with the money left her out of her mother's inheritance (from the African transactions of Mumford) and Robert's post-slavery savings, and in front of her picturesque little cottage spins yarns of her early experiences for the neighbors.

INTERVIEWED IN JACKSONVILLE,
JANUARY 11, 1937